American Minorities: The Justice Issue

ELTON LONG, J. D.   *Assistant Professor, Department of Criminal Justice, California State University, Sacramento*

JAMES LONG, J. D.   *Member of the California Bar Lecturer, California State University, Sacramento*

WILMER LEON   *Consultant, Intergroup Relations, California Department of Education Lecturer, California State University, Sacramento*

PAUL B. WESTON   *Professor, Department of Criminal Justice, California State University, Sacramento*

Prentice-Hall, Inc., Englewood Cliffs, New Jersey

Library of Congress Cataloging in Publication Data

Main entry under title:

American minorities.

    (Prentice-Hall essentials of law enforcement series)
    Bibliography: p.
    1. Criminal justice, Administration of—United
States. 2. Minorities—United States. 3. Prejudices
and antipathies. I. Long, Elton, 1943-
HV8138.A63   364.3   74-7321
ISBN 0-13-028118-2

Prentice-Hall Essentials of Law Enforcement Series
James D. Stinchcomb, Editor

© 1975 by Prentice-Hall, Inc.
Englewood Cliffs, New Jersey

10 9 8 7 6 5 4 3 2

Printed in the United States of America

Prentice-Hall International, Inc., *London*
Prentice-Hall of Australia, Pty. Ltd., *Sydney*
Prentice-Hall of Canada, Ltd., *Toronto*
Prentice-Hall of India Private Limited, *New Delhi*
Prentice-Hall of Japan, Inc., *Tokyo*

Contents

Preface

American Minorities: The Justice Issue describes the problems of the minority group victim of prejudice and discrimination in America. It traces the history of minority groups in white, Protestant American society from the conflicts of the native American Indian with early settlers. The problems of black Americans are probed, from the pre-Civil War Dred Scott case, the Jim Crow segregation laws, and the civil rights struggle to the 1954 desegregation of public education by the United States Supreme Court.

We will also deal with the private and official violence of rioters, Black Panthers, police, and prison guards and attempt to understand why and how minorities have received unjust and unequal treatment. By examining riots, confrontations, raids, shoot-outs, police-ghetto relations, the conditions of prisons, and the rights of prisoners, we will try to understand the complexity of the racial problems of the American criminal justice system.

In this study, the historical pattern emerges of a powerful majority group who have had more than a fair measure of control over the administration of justice in America. Black and brown populations living in ghettos and *barrios* continue to struggle for the equality guaranteed to all by the Fourteenth Amendment. The final chapters recommend solutions to these problems. They outline new antidiscrimination standards for police and corrections personnel and describe methods for improving police-community relations and the interaction of black and brown minorities with a white-dominated "establishment." Discussion questions and case references supplement each chapter to assist an in-depth examination of the problems and issues discussed in the text.

1

Introduction

No problem in America is more serious than that of minority groups being fairly treated by agencies and agents responsible for the administration of justice. Equitable treatment of minority groups by agents of criminal justice is more than a moral commitment; it is among the rights guaranteed to all citizens by the U.S. Constitution. The Fourteenth Amendment to the Constitution expresses the basic philosophy of American society, and its protection clause bars all discrimination because of race, creed, or previous condition of servitude; the Fifteenth Amendment prohibits denial or abridgement of the right to vote on the basis of race, creed, or previous service as a slave.

Law, from enactment to enforcement, is not an unknown vehicle for injustice to minority groups. The American Indian was an early victim. Immigrants contended with grossly unfair restrictions on their employment and citizenship. Black men and women fought the property rights inherent in the legal structure of slavery and, after slavery, they fought relegation to second-class citizenship. The Chinese were excluded from the United States by an act of Congress, and the Japanese in Western America were interned in relocation camps during World War II by executive order. The Mexican Americans of the Southwest were evicted from lands to which they had property rights, and were treated violently and imprisoned when they raised objections to government approval of the land confiscation. Federal and state power has been used against minorities to imprison persons, accuse them of crimes, and bring them before courts. The trials of such persons, however, were not in accordance with the basic constitutional guarantee of a fair trial before an impartial court.

The appellate courts have documented many cases of such injustice, and protest demonstrations have directed attention to many acts of inequity. A growing hostility to police activity on the part of many residents of ghettos housing black and Spanish-speaking populations has been joined by a rising militancy among black and brown prisoners protesting the processes of criminal justice which brought about their conviction and imprisonment.

These appeals, protests, and expressions of hostility and dissatisfaction have raised the profile of criminal justice in America and placed this area of social crisis before an increasingly aware public. Police action, criminal court trials, as well as unhealthy and unfair prison conditions, all of which suggest injustice toward minority groups, no longer have the protection of a low profile and public apathy. A new public interest in these areas is served by the news media which now consider such items newsworthy. A related public concern about unjust treatment of minority groups by elected and appointed public officials is also increasing.

A concerned public and its officials now realize that the violence of looting, arson, and attacks on police by ghetto residents; the wrecking of prisons by rioting inmates; and the ambushing of police by armed assailants stem from the lack of justice on the part of police, courts, and correctional personnel in their dealings with members of minority groups. In fact, there is a developing awareness that the violence of such actions is rooted in the frustrations of failure to achieve changes in the system.

To reduce the present incidence of injustice and the violent reactions to this condition, it is vital that all concerned with the administration of justice in America learn the complete facts about minority groups and criminal justice. When the problems are completely understood, it becomes apparent that pacification is not the answer to this violence; treatment of all people on an equal basis is the only solution, and a solution that cannot be long delayed.

THE EARLY YEARS—THE ANGLO-SAXON GROUP

Twentieth-century Americans differ socially and culturally because of their varied ethnic, racial, and national backgrounds, and their geographical separation over a vast country. In the early years of colonial America, the situation was quite different. The Anglo-Saxon group comprised the dominant majority in 1776, and, as the force behind the "establishment" in the early years, this group determined the main aspects of political and social life in the colonies.

The Angles originated in the district of Angle on the Danish peninsula. The Saxons inhabited the district between the Elbe and Weser Rivers. The name *Saxon* initially referred to an alliance of tribes that were users of the *seax* or *sahs*, a short one-handled sword. Settled in Britain by about the fifth century, the Angles and Saxons became so closely linked that they were referred to interchangeably. *Anglecynn* meant "English people," and their language was termed "English." By the mid-seventh century, the British mainland population was mainly Anglo-Saxon, with some migrants from Scandinavian and Germanic areas. Indigenous Britons were driven westward or absorbed into the Anglo-Saxon population.[1]

Normans—themselves of Danish ancestry—made a minor contribution to the Anglo-Saxon stock, especially the nobility. During the Reformation, thousands of refugees came to England from Europe. Genetically, an Anglo-Saxon is heterogeneous because the Anglo-Saxon world of early England absorbed Celts, Norse, Danes, and French.

The genealogy of colonial Americans is almost identical to that of the English, since in 1790 nearly two-thirds of the colonies' 3 million people were English. In the key states of Massachusetts and Virginia this ratio was even larger. Englishmen emigrated to America on a very large scale, assuming a predominant role in colonial affairs in the seventeenth century.

The colonists adapted Anglo-Saxon institutions to the environment of the New World and gradually emerged as the host society and core

---

[1]Charles H. Anderson, *White Protestant Americans: From National Origins to Religious Group* (Englewood Cliffs, N.J.: Prentice-Hall, 1970), pp. 13–14.

culture. New arrivals from England were quickly assimilated into colonial society. They simply adopted the American version of the Anglo-Saxon life styles of their own particular social status—professional, business, industrial, or agricultural.

PROTESTANTISM IN AMERICA

The colonial population was almost entirely Protestant. If any religion shaped the attitudes and behavior of early Americans and dominated early American institutions—consciously or unconsciously—it was Protestantism. Although the United States has never had an established state religion, Protestantism has often been accepted as an unspoken standard.

White Protestants in colonial America were basically Anglo-Saxon, but with several national origins: Welsh, English, Scottish, Scotch-Irish, Swedish, Norwegian, Finnish, Danish, German, and Dutch. Each of these groups was usually affiliated with one of the Protestant denominations: English with Episcopal (Anglican) and Congregational; Scottish with Presbyterian; Germans, Danes, Swedes, and Finns with Lutheran; and the Dutch with Reformed. Methodists and Baptists drew heavily from all national groups; many Protestants joined the most convenient local church. Despite these diverse national origins and some slight variance in religious views, American Protestants are linked closely with their Anglo-Saxon ancestry. *White Anglo-Saxon Protestant* (*WASP*) is a commonplace phrase in America.

In the 1830s, a majority of the nation's 13 million people identified themselves with some Protestant denomination. This religious feeling and identity probably reflected to a large degree the religious frenzy of revivalism, which swept the country in the early nineteenth century and made the Protestant church influential for generations to come.

American Catholics have, with varying degrees of intensity, always encountered the open opposition of many Protestants. Between periods of relative calm and outbursts of enmity, Protestants have typically viewed Catholics with palpable suspicion punctuated by fear. They have been suspicious of papal machinations against the democratic institutions of Protestant America. Anti-Catholicism has certainly not recovered its traditionally direct and overt style, but distrust, dislike, and abhorrence of Catholicism continue among substantial numbers of Protestants, especially within older generations. In all likelihood, many Protestants still consider Catholicism a "chief leader of alienism."[2]

[2]Anderson, *White Protestant Americans*, pp. 99–105.

NATIVISM

Nativism is a hardy perennial, and despite its political action program, *Know-Nothingism*, which died during the Civil War years, it came to full bloom again in the early 1890s as the American Protective Association (APA). The APA was born in Clinton, Iowa, in 1887. By 1893, it claimed a huge membership in twenty states, although exact figures were never made available. It was surprisingly strong in the Middle Western "Bible Belt," where the rapid growth of the Catholic Church had become alarming to nativists. The APA approved foreign-born people for citizenship if they believed in God and were not Roman Catholics. The APA planted the seed of its anti-Catholic and anti-foreign crusade in many bitter political campaigns, and the organization ousted Irish Catholics from city politics and jobs.

Because of the political and economic dissension and the general unrest of the times, the APA grew to its peak in 1893 and 1894. The anti-Catholic issue provided the emotional stimulus. Spurious documents, alleged papal encyclicals, were widely circulated. These purported papal decrees set the date when the Catholics should rise in one holy massacre to slay their Protestant neighbors. President Grover Cleveland was supposed to have had a private wire connecting the White House with the head of the Catholic hierarchy in America. The panic of 1893 was blamed on the Catholic religious order, the Jesuits. APA leaders claimed that the organization had nothing in its ritual against the "religious dogmas of any ecclesiastical corporation" and was not opposed to the foreign-born. However, these leaders admitted that the organization stressed the dangers of unlimited immigration and favored drastic restriction of immigrants and naturalization requirements ranging from seven to twenty-one years residence for citizenship.[3]

THE KU KLUX KLAN

The Ku Klux Klan (KKK) was formed in 1886 in the Reconstruction period which followed the defeat of the Southern Confederacy by Union forces in the Civil War. It was a secret terrorist organization, a resistance movement. Masked men in ghostly regalia usually rode at night, and a fiery cross was part of the Klan ritual. It was officially disbanded in 1869, revived in 1915, and more or less broken up in the

---

[3]Carl Wittke, *We Who Built America: The Saga of the Immigrant* (Cleveland, Ohio: Press of Case Western Reserve University, 1967, rev. ed. 1969), pp. 510–16.

following years. The stated objective of the KKK has long been to advocate the supremacy of white, male, native-born gentile citizens. It has always been hostile to Jews, Catholics, black Americans, and aliens.[4]

It is likely that the original Ku Klux Klan was a body of regulators or vigilantes attempting to cope with the social upheaval in the South caused by the Confederate surrender to the Union army. The emancipation of slaves and their integration into the Southern socioeconomic system under the direction of the victorious Northern forces made Southerners extremely uneasy.

Local option apparently allowed men of this extralegal organization to go about in disguise terrorizing some members of the community in the name of law enforcement. When the Klan was disbanded in 1869 its Grand Wizard stated that since the courts were now functioning properly and the local governments reestablished, there was no longer any need for the Klan's existence.[5]

Since local and national courts and government of the United States were functioning properly in 1915, the rebirth of the Ku Klux Klan cannot be justified by any claim that a vigilance committee was needed to preserve public order. Fraternity can justify any organization, of course, but when masks, disguises, and terrorizing are part of a group's ritual, and when the stated objective of the group seems to support hatred of nonwhites and non-Protestants, there is little justification in terming such a group a "fraternal" organization. Mob violence by groups claiming KKK allegiance pointed to the revived Ku Klux Klan as a hate group.

WHITE CITIZENS' COUNCIL

In 1954, the U.S. Supreme Court's desegregation of public schools led to the establishment of White Citizens' Councils (WCC) in Mississippi. Overtly dedicated to maintaining peace, good order, and domestic tranquility and to preserving states' rights, the WCC movement quickly spread to many states in the Black Belt, particularly Texas, Arkansas, Alabama, Georgia, and South Carolina. It was a resistance movement organized as a federation of independent local groups. Its major stated objective was to fight integration in the public schools; weapons were

---

[4]Stanley Frost, *The Challenge of the Klan* (Westport, Conn.: Greenwood Press, 1969; originally published in 1924 by Bobbs-Merrill), pp. 57–59, 94–97.

[5]Henry P. Fry, *The Modern Ku Klux Klan* (Westport, Conn.: Greenwood Press, 1969; originally published in 1922 by Small, Maynard), pp. 135–36.

economic and social pressure.[6] Its unstated purpose was the broader objective of keeping blacks in the role of laborer and allowing no integration of blacks into the social system. Since some of the area's leading businessmen and landowners were members of the WCC, such economic pressure significantly hurt the livelihood of the black population comprising the local labor group as well as the white residents who failed to cooperate with the WCC.

In theory, social, economic, and political pressures can achieve objectives without overt violence, but hot-headed, angry men exist in any organization, and thus there is always a potential for violence should one of these groups confront someone who fails to submit to the group's more subtle pressures. An inherent danger in an organization such as the WCC is that it may become a "night-riding, sheeted mob, terrorizing selected persons in the community" in the image of the Ku Klux Klan.[7]

The activity of White Citizens' Councils led to a new structure of violence in the South. Demonstrators protesting the failure of southern schools to desegregate in accordance with the United States Supreme Court's direction in *Brown* v. *Board of Education*,[8] were beaten; the homes of integrationists were bombed; and police officers killed or wounded blacks in various segregation-desegregation conflicts.

LYNCHINGS

Lynchings occur chiefly when discrimination and segregation are firmly entrenched, where the separation of the races is customarily enforced by severe intimidation, and where there is a low level of law enforcement in the community. The fact that lynchings are not prevented, and even known lynchers are not apprehended, reflects the silent approval of community, police, and prosecutor.

Two types of lynching have been distinguished. The first is the *vigilante* lynching. The victim is accused of a crime, apprehended by a small, well-ordered band of citizens, and lynched quietly. The second is the *mob* lynching, which is marked generally by ferocity and bestial-

[6]Harold C. Fleming, "Resistance Movements and Racial Desegregation," *The Annals of the American Academy of Political and Social Science,* Vol. 304, March 1956, pp. 44–52.

[7]Hodding Carter, "A Wave of Terror Threatens the South," *Look,* Vol. 16, No. 6, March 22, 1955, pp. 32–36.

[8]347 U.S. 483 (1954).

ity. Sometimes, the resultant torture of the victim and mutilation of the corpse are excessive and revolting.[9]

Because there were few courthouses in the American colonies, vigilante pursuits of offenders and summary punishments were a useful social control. Judge Lynch, whose name is identified with these crimes, was a Virginia Quaker. During the American Revolution Tories were caught stealing horses. As magistrate he set up court in his own home and rapidly sentenced the thieves to forty lashes. His own religious scruples forbade him taking human life.

This whole practice depended considerably on cultural custom. In certain localities there was a tradition of a manhunt as a duty, and local law-enforcement authorities exhibited a lenient attitude toward this tradition. Over the years, however, this rough, frontier justice was buried by the racial discrimination seeking revenge in murder.

From 1882 to 1951, excluding the post-Civil War years and the nation's frontier period, two and a half times as many blacks as whites were executed by lynching. Mississippi, Georgia, and Texas outranked all other states in the incidence of lynchings. Since the turn of the century lynchings diminished from over a hundred a year to a single lynching in 1951.[10]

In 1945, the U.S. Supreme Court ruled that lynching was a deprivation of life without due process of law when police were involved in the lynching. The Court's opinion in *Screws* v. *United States*[11] notes, "This case involves a shocking and revolting episode in law enforcement."[12] Sheriff Screws of Baker County, Georgia, enlisted the assistance of a local policeman and a special deputy to arrest Robert Hall, a young black about thirty years old, for the theft of an automobile tire. Hall was arrested in his home under the authority of a warrant secured by Sheriff Screws, was handcuffed and taken by car to the courthouse. When Hall alighted from the car in the courthouse square, the three arresting officers began beating him with their fists and a solid-bar blackjack about eight inches long and weighing two pounds. Hall fell to the ground, still handcuffed, and the officers continued to beat him for fifteen to thirty minutes until he was unconscious. Hall was then dragged feet first through the courthouse square into the jail in the basement of the courthouse and thrown upon the floor. Later, an ambu-

[9]Gordon W. Allport, *The Nature of Prejudice* (Reading, Mass.: Addison-Wesley, 1954), pp. 61–63.

[10]Jessie Parkhurst Guyman, "Lynching," *Racial Violence in the United States* (Chicago: Aldine, 1969), pp. 56–59.

[11]325 U.S. 91 (1945).

[12]*Screws* v. *United States*, 325 U.S. 91 (1945), p. 92.

lance removed Hall to the local hospital where he died within the hour without regaining consciousness.

Sheriff Screws claimed Hall reached for a gun and cursed him when he alighted from the car. Evidence presented at the trial indicated the three defendants had previously threatened to kill Hall, fortified themselves at a nearby bar, and resisted the bartender's urgent requests not to carry out the arrest.[13]

Sheriff Screws and his two assisting officers were convicted of violating Section 20 of the United States Criminal Code (i.e., of having willfully deprived a person of any right secured to him by the due process clause of the Fourteenth Amendment). The problem in *Screws* was not whether state law had been violated, but whether an inhabitant of a state has been deprived of a federal right by one who acts under color of official right. As the Court's opinion noted: "Section 20 was enacted to enforce the Fourteenth Amendment. It derives from Section 2 of the Civil Rights Act of April 9, 1866. ... Its purpose was to protect all persons in the United States in their civil rights and furnish the means of their vindication."[14]

Although Sheriff Screws and his two police associates could have been tried for criminal homicide and found guilty of manslaughter or murder under state law, no local action was taken in this case. The federal government could prosecute only on a relatively minor charge related to depriving victim Hall of a constitutional right—life. Since Hall's killing was a criminal homicide only under state law, the federal government could not prosecute the killers for taking life.

Lynching of blacks by a white mob with or without police involvement may be a relic of the past, but it is apparent that action by the federal government is unlikely to deter such tragic behavior. As in the past, lynchings will occur because the lynch mob does not fear prosecution under state law.

SECTIONALISM

Sectionalism is found in areas where residents hold common attitudes and behave in a unique manner which is quite different from the attitudes and behavior of residents in another section. In addition, sectional attitudes and behavior tend to perpetuate themselves; when residents of one section move to a new section, they tend to retain the old attitudes.

[13]*Screws* v. *United States*, p. 113.
[14]*Screws* v. *U.S.*, p. 98.

Geographical factors, ethnic background, and the national origins of certain populations were the fundamental factors in establishing sections in colonial America. In the middle of the eighteenth century it was proposed that the English colonies in America be divided into three countries, *North, Middle,* and *South.* This early recognition of the Yankee, non-Yankee, and southern sections along the Eastern seaboard foreshadowed the sectional differences which persisted despite joinder into a federal union in 1776.[15] (See map 1.)

Common national feeling held these sections together until the dispute over slavery arose. Until this time, lateral migration had carried the spheres of influence of the three seaboard sections inland across the Mississippi valley to the West. Rivalry between slave and nonslave sections widened the gap between the North and the South and turned the middle or non-Yankee area into a border area with sympathy divided between North and South.

Divergent viewpoints on the slavery issue became a basic controversy of black versus white, and the best example of sectionalism in the United States is found in the difference between southern attitudes towards this issue and those of other sections of the country. The *South* may be defined as the states that seceded from the Union to form the Confederacy (Virginia, North Carolina, South Carolina, Tennessee, Georgia, Alabama, Florida, Mississippi, Arkansas, Louisiana, and Texas). This definition may be extended to the so-called border states as an *Outer South* (Delaware, Maryland, West Virginia, Kentucky, Missouri, and Oklahoma). The attitudes and behavior of the residents of these border states are similar to those of the south. Much of the border state population migrated from states in the South; some of these states seceded from the Union to join the Confederacy; and their state legislatures enacted racial segregation laws similar to those in the South.[16] (See map 2.)

In post-Civil War years, loyalty to the Yankee or Confederate cause divided the new states carved out of America's heartland, the Southwest and Pacific areas. This division along Civil War lines identified the Border (Outer South), Central and Southwest states with the Confederate cause, and the Great Lakes, Farm Belt, and Northern Rocky Mountain states with the northern forces. Similarly, on the Pacific Coast, the northern area was an extension of the Yankee environment, while the

[15]Frederick Jackson Turner, *The Significance of Sections in American History* (Gloucester, Mass.: Peter Smith, 1959; originally published in 1932 by Henry Holt), pp. 288–309.

[16]Ira Sharkansky, *Regionalism in American Politics* (Indianapolis, Ind.: Bobbs-Merrill, 1970), pp. 165–66, 169–73.

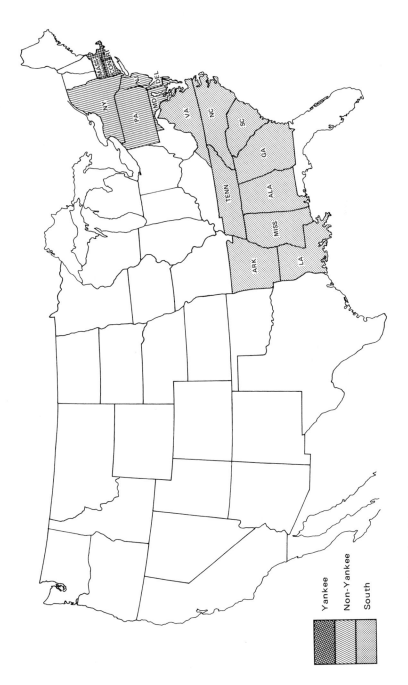

Map 1. Origins of Sectionalism

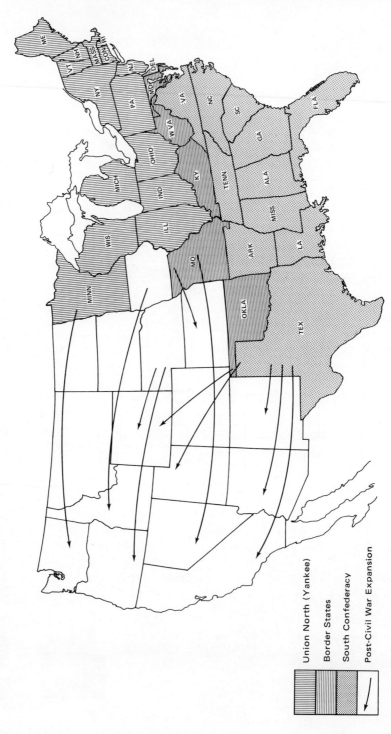

Map 2. Expansion of Sectionalism—Civil War Years

Union North (Yankee)

Border States

South Confederacy

Post-Civil War Expansion

central and southern areas were settled by a mixed group of southerners, non-Yankees, and Yankees, all with various wartime biases developed during the strife of 1861 to 1865. In effect, the Civil War dictated social and political loyalties in many sections of the United States for the next century.[17]

In 1900 roughly nine million blacks lived in the United States, and almost eight million lived in the South under a traditional pattern of white supremacy: the lines of authority were clearly drawn, and the power of the white community was overwhelming. At that time only 385,000 blacks lived in the northeastern states, 496,000 were residents of the north central section, and only 30,000 called the western area their home.

In 1920, the Great Migration to the cities of the Northeast and Northwest began, and the southern states had a net loss of 122,000 blacks. By 1929 the South had lost a total of 520,000 black inhabitants. In 1930, the major migratory trend in the United States was from the Southeast (3,412,150 residents) into the Southwest and Far West. To a lesser extent, the Northeast and Middle States contributed to this movement (632,452 residents), and to an increased population in the Northwest (1,072,376 residents).[18]

The states of the South and Outer South comprise a massive section of the United States commonly called the "Black Belt." It extends from Virginia to Texas, and its central area is the heartland of the southern slave states. Since residents of the South and Outer South states migrate northward and westward, this section also exports discrimination and prejudice, basic tenets of the sectional attitude toward white supremacy.

In addition, the immigration of Europeans, Orientals, and Spanish-speaking people, and their spread from the East and West coasts inward, and from the Mexican border northward, has further balkanized the classic sections of the United States.[19] As a result, minority groups differ in size and composition, as does the white dominant group.

Ancestors of the white Anglo-Saxon Protestants who comprise our dominant population group now face a racial problem which is even more complex than the original issue of slavery. The basic problem of

---

[17]Kevin P. Phillips, *The Emerging Republican Majority* (New Rochelle, N.Y.: Arlington House, 1969), pp. 93–96.

[18]Howard W. Odum and Harry Estell Moore, *American Regionalism: A Cultural-Historical Approach to National Integration* (Gloucester, Mass.: Peter Smith, 1966), pp. 449–81.

[19]The Balkan states of Southern Europe have a long history of armed disputes among themselves, hence *balkanization* refers to the process of breaking up a region into smaller, often hostile, units.

blacks and browns in conflict with the white population which led to nativism, the Klan, White Citizens' Councils, lynching, and other violence can be solved only by equal and just treatment under law for all people; but these goals must be achieved in states made up of many enclaves that are similar but different.

The strength of sectionalism is indicated by the resistance of an area to national uniformity (as the South exhibited in its struggle against the North over the slavery issue), and by the unique mental and emotional attitudes which separate the area from other sections, or the nation as a whole. Sectionalism unites groups of states with similar social, economic, and political stances. Thus, statewide policy may conflict with that of other states or with the policy of the central government; and some hostility is necessarily associated with these differences.

LOCAL OPTION AND FEDERAL POWER

Local government affects the ordinary citizen far more than any federal agents or agencies. Government at the local level consists of: the municipality's police, the sheriff and his deputies within a county, the county prosecutor or district attorney, the local judiciary, and the local residents who serve as grand or trial jurors.

From experience, minorities look on these city, county, and state agents as reflections of local options in law enforcement. Local enforcement may not be in harmony with enforcement in other sections or in accordance with federal government guidelines and constitutional guarantees. Therefore, minorities in some areas tend to regard these agents of local justice not as protectors but as persons to be feared, because the authority to arrest, to bail, to prosecute, or to adjudicate may be exercised in a way which denies minorities equal protection of the law. Minorities who "know their place" are not troubled; but those who insist on their rights as citizens of the United States find that the local option intimidates and discourages citizens attempting to escape from their subordinate role.

Failure of local law enforcement and criminal justice agents to curb racial violence has resulted in direct use of federal power to protect the rights of minorities. Such action is within the letter and intent of Article VI of the United States Constitution which proclaims federal law the "supreme law of the land." In 1963, during the civil rights disturbances in Birmingham, Alabama, President John F. Kennedy reminded Alabama's governor that Congress had entrusted to the President the right to determine the necessity of federal force to prevent or suppress violence, the means to be employed, and the adequacy of the protection afforded by the state authorities to its citizens. Later, the U.S. Department of Justice informed the Supreme Court that such presidential intervention was justified whenever violence, or an unlawful combination or conspiracy, so hinders the ordinary process of law enforcement that a part or class of people is deprived of federal constitutional rights, including the right of equal protection of the laws, which the state authorities are unable, fail, or refuse to protect.[20]

Unfortunately, prosecutors, sheriffs, and other peace officers who have personal or political reasons for refusing minorities equal protection and due process of the law can generally follow their prejudices without interference. Federal power is used only when the event is so brutal and shocking that refusal of local authorities to prosecute indicates gross injustice on racial grounds.

THE GHETTO

Ghetto was originally the name of the Jewish quarter of sixteenth-century Venice. Later it was used to designate the section of any city in which Jews were confined. In America it came to mean an area in which any minority was confined: a separate and subordinate colony usually characterized by overcrowding, deteriorated housing, and poverty.[21] This residential segregation isolates the minority from the dominant community and, in general, makes it difficult or impossible for ghetto residents to move up and out of the ghetto.

In the past voluntary segregation formed some ghettos, but it is equally true—then and now—that poverty and discrimination have locked minorities into slum areas. Rent, when calculated per units of square feet, is high; only when it is calculated per units of population can this high-density housing be termed "low-rent." Because they are involuntarily segregated into "low-rent" areas, minorities are forced to pay for the crowded housing. Restrictive covenants written into deeds transferring the titles to residential housing have been the formal means of exclusion; claims that tenancy by racial minorities lowers real estate values or income from rental properties foster informal discrimination.

Many believe the fiction that members of minority groups want to live together in a neighborhood and that their inability to pay nominal rents forces them to reside in a low-rent area. In reality, minorities are forced to live in ghettos because they are not wanted in other areas.

[20]*Alabama* v. *U.S.*, 373 U.S. 545 (1963).

[21]Kenneth B. Clark, *Dark Ghetto: Dilemmas of Social Power* (New York: Harper & Row, 1965), pp. 11–12.

As an adaptive device for introducing foreign-born immigrants to the so-called American way of life, the ethnic ghettos served a useful purpose. New settlers found others from a similar background, newspapers in their native language, and storekeepers who understood their language, and ghettos such as the Irish Shantytowns, the German urban neighborhoods, the Little Italys, the Chinatowns, and the Little Tokyos served as a threshold to the new life and unfamiliar language. Some of the early arrivals moved out of the ghetto, and were replaced by immigrants of their own ethnic group and eventually by those of another group.

For example, slum housing on New York's East Side (Manhattan) was first populated by Irish immigrants. Several sections were then populated by Germans (Yorkville), by Italians (Little Italy), and by Chinese (Chinatown). Since New York is on the East Coast, Japanese Americans did not settle there to any great extent. Later, when New York was the focus of the black migration from the South, the same area became a black ghetto; Puerto Ricans then migrated from their homeland and took over block after block of the same area. The transition of ethnic groups, including the recently arrived Puerto Rican group, usually spanned no more than one generation, but the black ghetto population has been in this area since before World War I. The black racial ghetto, unlike an ethnic ghetto, is not an adaptive device, but a residential segregation which reduces the racial minority population to an isolated and subordinate status.

Historically, ghetto schools have effectively killed their students' desire to learn. Physical plants are old and run-down; instructional staff are hostile, bitter, or incompetent. In addition, instruction is keyed to a common belief that ghetto youngsters have difficulty in learning and are inferior to nonghetto students.

Dropouts are common; "pushouts" are equally common. Both procedures promote ghetto students without the knowledge common to those at the same scholastic levels in nonghetto schools. The growth of vocational and continuation schools in black ghettos illustrates the failure of education in ghetto areas. These schools do little more than house students on school days. Reading levels are not improved, and students are not prepared for any further education. The lack of bilingual schools in the Spanish-speaking *barrios* of the Southwest indicates a similar failure in the basic educational system.

Racial ghettos have invisible walls which are as confining as real walls in the restrictions they place on the lives of those inside them. The ghetto child is held back in his search for an education, and men and women are crippled in their search for employment. Moreover, ghetto walls block communication between those behind them and those living outside; the dominant majority is thus insulated against the plight of those in the ghetto.

PATTERNS OF MINORITY RELATIONS

Four historical patterns of minority relations with the dominant population group account for present problems with minority groups in various states and sections of the United States: (1) colonial settlement; (2) political annexation; (3) immigration; (4) slavery.[22]

The colonial pattern enabled early settlers in America to develop a trading economy with the natives. Sometimes, as in the early Indian wars, the settlers used force to establish political control and subordinate the Indian population. Social barriers were rigid; the color line between the white dominant population and the red men and women was fundamental, and half-breeds, usually with a white father and an Indian mother, were rejected by the white dominant group because of their Indian blood.

The political annexation pattern led to problems in the southwestern United States. When our border with Mexico was re-aligned to place land formerly part of Mexico within the boundaries of the United States, residents of these lands became a minority, and both social and economic discrimination by the dominant group resulted. The Mexican Americans differed in their native language, their appearance, and their cultural heritage. They were rejected because of these differences, and for many years any person of Mexican origin who moved north of the border was ostracized.

The immigration pattern has been identified with discrimination against Irish, Orientals, and Jews in many sections of the country. Dislike of the Irish immigrants arose because they differed from the native-born American colonials. They were poor, not wealthy or even self-supporting; they were identified with strong drink, not with temperance; they were believed criminally inclined, rather than law-abiding; and they spoke with a strange accent different from the proper British one. While their biological features were similar to those of the dominant group, the Irish were readily identifiable by their cultural and associational features.

Hostility to Orientals originally centered on the Chinese. They differed in appearance because of their almond-shaped eyes, and early immigrants wore their hair in a long braid, the traditional queue. They

[22]Charles F. Marden and Gladys Meyer, *Minorities in American Society*, 2nd ed. (New York: American Book, 1962), p. 6.

had difficulty in speaking English and maintained their cultural and associational visibility. *Coolie labor* was a disparaging term used to describe Chinese immigrants who worked at substandard salary levels; social discrimination relegated the Chinese to occupational roles such as cooks and laundrymen. Later, Japanese immigrants encountered similar discrimination, despite their basic competence to perform skilled labor and to handle executive responsibility. Their success in competition with members of the dominant group probably accounts for the internment of this minority during World War II, following the Japanese nation's attack on Pearl Harbor.

Jews of many nationalities were discriminated against because of their nonconforming religion. Jewish immigrants of a particular nationality found less acceptance by the dominant group than did gentile immigrants of the same nationality. The hyphenated identification, such as "German-Jews" rather than "Germans," indicated rejection based on religion rather than nationality.

The slavery pattern affects the black minority in America. African natives were imported to colonial America as early as 1619. From its origins in 1776, the United States held a slave minority in subservience by law. A bitterly contested war made slavery illegal, and the Constitution was amended to grant the freed slaves full citizenship. Segregation of this easily identified minority led to occupational, social, and political discrimination much greater than discrimination of other minorities resulting from the colonial, the political annexation, or the immigration patterns.

The colonial pattern left contemporary America with a disadvantaged minority group, the American Indians. The political annexation pattern developed a major discrimination problem in the Southwest with the Mexican Americans or Chicanos, and created problems involving the Puerto Rican migrants when the United States took over their island. The immigration pattern created transient problems during the eras of European immigration, contributed to the exclusion of Oriental immigrants and the mistreatment of the Japanese during World War II, and opened the United States as a refuge for Cuban nationals who fled when the Castro government seized power. The slavery pattern left this country with the racial problem of a white dominant majority group and a black minority population.

DISCUSSION QUESTIONS

1. What is the origin of the American WASP?
2. What are the basic characteristics of hate groups in America?

3. Explain the concept of sectionalism. Are lynchings related to sectionalism? How?
4. Can federal power overcome the "local option" inherent in sectionalism? How?
5. What are the patterns of minority relations which led to contemporary discrimination against minorities?

CASE REFERENCES

Alabama v. *United States,* 373 U.S. 545 (1963).
Screws v. *United States,* 325 U.S. 91 (1945).

2

Disadvantaged Minorities in America

INDIANS
MEXICAN AMERICANS
PUERTO RICANS
CUBANS
BLACKS

A United States citizen is often referred to simply as an "American." Ethnically and in natural law, however, the only true Americans are the descendants of the American Indians, natives of North and South America.

A disadvantaged minority group in the United States can be defined as a group of native Americans, immigrants, migrants, or refugees who are victims of the dominant white population's prejudice and discrimination, and who are handicapped by race or language and the lack of ethnic, family, and socioeconomic resources. The American Indians, Mexican Americans, and the Puerto Ricans, Cubans, and blacks living in America are disadvantaged minorities.

INDIANS

American Indians did not give up their land without a struggle. In the early days they fought to oust the settlers; then they battled to retain
20

enough of their tribal lands to support their food-gathering economy; finally they resisted enclosure on reservations. In 1645, Virginia garrisoned a chain of forts to fight off the Indians; in the Pequot War of 1636, a Massachusetts militia ousted an Indian tribe from its lands and thus opened up the inland areas of New England to settlement; in 1786, Ohio tribesmen attacked traders and raided settlements in defiance of the new United States government.

Military supremacy achieved, the new nation entered the second stage of subordinating the Indians: signing agreements and "treaties" that surrendered Indian lands. After opening these lands for settlement, settlers clashed with Indians and forced them into small reserved areas of their former vast landholdings. Demand for land, however, spurred the federal government's decision for "removal" of the Indians to unwanted lands West of the Mississippi. Black Hawk, chief of the Winnebago tribe, led his followers across the Mississippi only when faced with 1,500 Illinois militiamen. Later, unhappy over the "bargain" forced on him, Black Hawk led 1,000 Indians back to their homeland. They were trapped between land and a gunboat in the Mississippi, driven back into the river, and slaughtered as they retreated across the wide waters. About 150 Indians survived and were taken as prisoners.[1]

The ruthlessness exhibited against Black Hawk and his Winnebago followers was no doubt a contributing factor in later agreements of Indian tribes to move west of the Mississippi. When a particular group of Indians showed any reluctance, federal troops "escorted" them west.

In 1830 Congress formalized this procedure, authorizing the President to move any eastern tribe west across the Mississippi to an assigned area and to use military force if necessary. The Seminole War defeated the last major group of Indians resisting westward removal. When the last of the Seminoles were defeated and escorted westward by 1842, all the natives formerly of the eastern United States were now residents of a vast ghetto-like area in the West and Far West.[2]

The Cherokee tribe of Georgia, termed the "Cherokee Nation," asked the U.S. Supreme Court in 1830 to intervene on their behalf and to prevent state agents from harrassing them and taking possession of their lands. In *Cherokee Nation* v. *Georgia*,[3] their plea was rejected, and they were soon ousted and started on the long trip west.

Resettling the Indians failed to resolve the problem of white relations with Indians. The West and Far West were opened to settlement, cattlemen moved up from Texas, and farming families crossed the Missis-

[1]Ray Allen Billington, *Westward Expansion: A History of the American Frontier*, 2nd ed. (New York: Macmillan, 1960), pp. 297–301.

[2]Billington, *Westward Expansion*, pp. 315–17.

[3]30 U.S. (Peters 5) 1 (1831).

sippi. Gold was discovered in California, and white hunters killed the buffalo that had been a staple of the Indian diet. Again, white settlers, cattlemen, and miners fought with the Indians. This time there were fewer Indians to be moved, as a result of armed conflicts and hunger. Smaller areas were designated for the displaced Indians. These reservations offered some chance of survival despite the slaughter of the buffalo but were usually located in areas unwanted by the land-hungry whites. Unlike the Irish, German, and Italian immigrants who left their homeland hoping to obtain individual liberty or to escape poverty the Indians were forced out of their homeland into barren lands where physical survival itself was difficult.

After subjugating the Indians by military force, and segregating them on reservations, the federal government made the Indian population wards by congressional action in 1871. In 1887, the Dawes Act established a new land policy to encourage Indians to work their own plots of land. This land allotment policy failed, as did the government's attempt to teach Indians the "American" way: the competitive success-oriented culture of the dominant group.

The Citizenship Act of 1924 conferred United States and state citizenship on all Indians. State services to Indians have increased since 1924 and the states have developed a positive view of their responsibilities. In 1934, the Indian Reorganization Act sought new directions: to integrate Indians into American life as persons with a rich cultural heritage. To date, Indians have been subordinated and ghettoized, and though most have mastered English, they have not been successful in escaping from their subordinate status.[4]

MEXICAN AMERICANS

Before 1910, people of Mexican ancestry who had lived along the border of the Southwest territories before their annexation formed most of the Mexican American population in the United States. (See map 3). From 1910 to 1920 the Mexican revolution fostered the first substantial movement of people north from Mexico, and potential job opportunities made immigration attractive to Mexican nationals. World War I and its manpower requirements forced ranchers and growers in the Southwest to depend on Mexican American labor and temporary farm workers imported from Mexico.

Immigration from Mexico reached its peak in the years from 1920 to 1930. This migration caused concern in Mexico over the loss to the

[4]Marden and Meyer, *Minorities in American Society*, pp. 326–51.

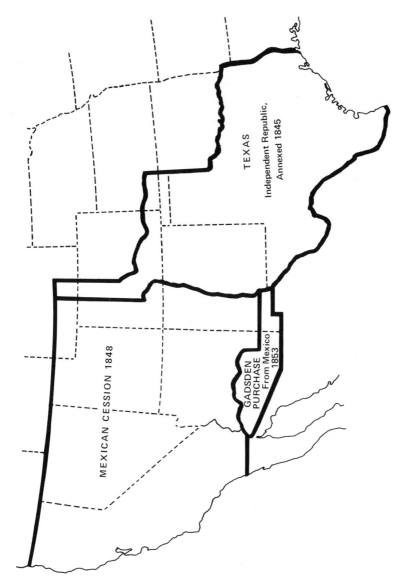

Map 3. Origins of Mexican Americans—Mexico and the American Southwest

Mexican labor force and fear in the United States concerning this new "foreigner" in its labor market. During the depression years (1929–1939), there was a decline of Mexican immigration and a return of Mexican Americans to their homeland. Some returned because of the bleak employment situation in the United States; others were returned by immigration authorities because of suspected illegal entry into the country, although high unemployment was probably the real cause of this strict enforcement program.

Data on the net Mexican immigration from 1920 to 1939 illustrates this ebb and flow northward:[5]

Year	Net Immigration
1920	44,436
1925	29,424
1930	5,560
1935	–5,488
1939	–2,852

The threat of military conscription during World War II curtailed Mexican immigration for the years from 1940 to 1949. Permanent-visa immigration totaled only 54,500 for this decade: 16,500 from 1940 to 1944; 38,000 for the years from 1945 to 1949.

However, from 1950 to 1960 over a quarter million immigrants arrived from Mexico in the United States.[6] During World War II the United States and Mexico initiated the bracero program: recruitment and transport of agricultural labor under the conditions of a government treaty between nations. The shortage of farm and ranch help during the war and the concurrent lack of voluntary immigration resulted in this emergency action, but the program did not end until December, 1964.[7] This program gave Mexican nationals an opportunity to view American life in the Southwest.

On their return to Mexico many of these workers applied for permanent visas to return to the United States; others remained in the United States or returned to the United States as illegal aliens. Many Mexican nationals did not want to devote the time and money for the fees and commissions needed to obtain a permanent visa or a place in the bracero program; these people were called "wetbacks" because one

[5]Leo Grebler, *Mexican Immigration to the United States: Advance Report 2* (Los Angeles, Univ. of Ca., 1966), pp. 17–25.

[6]Grebler, *Mexican Immigration to the U.S.* pp. 29–34.

[7]Grebler, *Mexican Immigration to the U.S.* pp. 25–29.

easy entry was to swim the Rio Grande river which formed a major portion of the United States-Mexican boundary.

Whether the braceros led to the wetbacks, or the great number of wetbacks entering the United States for ranch and farm work led to an official program for temporary admission of agricultural workers is not known. Both movements satisfied the growers and ranchers in the United States as well as the Mexican workers. Through the illegal route, Mexican laborers had to pay fewer government and labor contractors's fees and avoided the red tape of government operations and supervision.

From 1953 to 1956, the American government struggled to expel the wetbacks from the Southwest. Many of the illegal immigrants had lived and worked in the United States for years, and many of their children were born here. This mass repatriation of Mexicans resembled a massive roundup in the manhunt tradition of the western frontier; no such disruption of employment, family, housing, and kinship ties is ever gentle or considerate. The great number of people apprehended and deported during the years of this operation indicates the scope of this roundup:[8]

Year	Number of Apprehensions
1953	875,000
1954	1,035,282
1955	256,290
1956	90,122

More recently, a government commuter program for the entry of Mexican agriculture labor into the United States for a day or a short period has replaced the braceros and, to some extent, the wetbacks. A major problem with this program is that this ready flow of labor willing to work for low wages has been used to combat agricultural labor unions in the Southwest. When Mexican American labor unions strike to gain higher wages and other benefits, the farmers and growers have locked out American workers and imported a commuter labor force to work the fields under local police protection. Domestic tranquility is preserved although this "sweetheart" arrangement between labor and management is not possible in other labor disputes and has become a device, as were the braceros, to threaten and to subordinate a minority group.[9]

[8]Grebler, *Mexican Immigration to the U.S.*, p. 34.

[9]Reuben Salazar, *Stranger in One's Land* (Washington, D.C.: Superintendent of Documents, 1970), pp. 11–15.

Mexican Americans are the country's second largest minority. They are primarily Catholics, and, although classed ethnically as whites of Mexican ancestry, Mexican Americans are not thought of as fellow Caucasians by the white dominant group in the United States. The Mexican ethnic heritage relates more closely to the Spanish conquerors and the Indians of Mexico and the Southwest than to the American white culture. Mexican Americans are sometimes identified as "brown" because of their olive-to-dark complexions; their visibility as a minority is heightened by their native language, Spanish.

When the United States gained the Southwest from Mexico by force of arms, this southward extension of our border was formalized in the 1848 Treaty of Guadalupe-Hidalgo. This treaty guaranteed that the property and political life of the native Mexican population would be protected. Over the ensuing years, however, the dominant non-Mexican population group has gained complete control of agriculture, commerce, and industry in the Southwest, and native Mexicans and generations of their children have been reduced to the role of a conquered people living in ghetto-like *barrios* and exhibiting the apathy, passivity, and indifference common to a conquered population.[10]

The Mexican American minority is heavily concentrated in five southwestern states: Texas, Arizona, New Mexico, Colorado, and California. For many years, Texas was their preferred area, but California is now the most popular state. Concentration of this minority in such proximity to their homeland is largely related to the similarities of climate and terrain to their native land, to the opportunity to meet other Spanish-speaking people, and to the level of poverty that precludes movement to unknown areas with uncertain employment opportunities. The recent popularity of California as a place of residence is probably because of the possibilities it seems to offer for improved social and economic conditions.

PUERTO RICANS

Persons moving from Puerto Rico, an American possession, to the United States are a twentieth century wave of United States citizens fleeing their homeland to improve their economic status, and they are immigrants rather than migrants.

The Puerto Rican immigrants settled in large urban areas in the East (eighty percent in New York City) and in midwestern cities. Because they are usually unskilled in any occupation, their occupational mobility has been limited, and they have had to take poorly paying jobs until

---

[10]Salazar, *Stranger in One's Land*, pp. 23–29.

they become skilled workers. Most of these immigrants have little facility in the English language, and, because many Puerto Ricans are biologically identifiable by dark skins, they encounter similar difficulties to those encountered by blacks.[11]

Before World War II, about seventy percent of the Puerto Ricans in New York City were listed as "Negro," and at that time the Puerto Rican census listed a slightly smaller percentage of the total population as "colored." Skin color in Puerto Rico ranges from white, through intermediate ranges, to black. Darker skin colors among Puerto Ricans are identified with low socioeconomic status, less education, and little upward social-economic mobility. As the migration from Puerto Rico continued, however, more immigrants were from the middle- and upper-income levels, and the percentage of "whites"—those who claim a pure Spanish lineage—is much higher as the family income level rises.[12]

The native language is not the only Spanish cultural tie the Puerto Ricans have. Spain settled the island in the sixteenth century; America did not take its government over until 1898. The present generation of islanders, however, view themselves as Puerto Rican Americans, enjoying unrestricted movement between the home island and the mainland because Puerto Ricans are United States citizens.[13]

The promise of future career opportunities in New York led many Puerto Ricans to flee the overpopulation and unemployment of their island home. The immigration pattern from Puerto Rico began to increase shortly after World War I. Oceangoing ships terminating in New York City brought the bulk of the immigrants to their new mainland homes. From 1929 to 1934, immigration slowed because of America's economic problems during the depression. Preparation for World War II brought economic prosperity to industry in the United States at the same time that the drafting of civilians for military service was reducing the available labor; many immigrants came to the mainland to fill these vacant jobs.

As these immigrants established themselves, they sent for friends and relatives, and the Puerto Rican American population grew. In 1950,

[11]J. Milton Yinger and George E. Simpson, "The Integration of Americans of Mexican, Puerto Rican and Oriental Descent," *The Annals of the American Academy of Political and Social Science,* Vol. 304, March 1956, pp. 127–29.

[12]Nathan Glazer and Daniel P. Moynihan, *Beyond the Melting Pot: The Negroes, Puerto Ricans, Jews, Italians, and Irish of New York City* (Cambridge, Mass. The M.I.T. Press, 1963), pp. 130–34.

[13]Charles W. Mills, Clarence Senior, and Rose K. Goldsen, *The Puerto Rican Journey: New York's Newest Migrants* (New York: Russell & Russell, 1967; orig. pub. in 1950 by Harper & Bros.), pp. 3–21.

the Puerto Rican population in the U.S. was 83,000; in 1955 it doubled to a total of 166,000.[14] Earlier immigrants have moved out of ghetto areas while maintaining contacts with their Spanish culture and the Spanish-speaking world. Many, however, have not yet moved out; large families, low incomes, the high costs of ghetto living, and failure of children to succeed in English-speaking public schools have blocked such upward mobility. While many of the earlier immigrants have the funds to move out of the ghetto, they remain because of the ownership of many small stores. The bodegas, small grocery stores which characterize most Puerto Rican ghettos, illustrate the shopkeeping ability of the Puerto Ricans.

CUBANS

The Cubans who fled from the fall of the Batista government in 1958 are not immigrants as much as they are refugees—persons displaced by a government they hated and feared. This movement of people was motivated largely by pressure to leave Cuba, rather than the attraction of a better life in the United States.

Refugees or exiles, the Cubans may be compared to a persecuted minority who immigrated because a dominant group harrassed them at home. These people, however, were not a minority group in Cuba; they were a fair cross section of the general Cuban population, except for their united opposition to the rule of a new government.[15] Like the Puerto Ricans, they became a minority in America because of their visibility: olive-to-dark skins, Spanish as a native language, and a unique culture.

The exodus of Cuban refugees seeking asylum in the United States did not reach substantial proportion until 1960. In 1961 and 1962, the intake of these refugees continued under funding from various federal public assistance acts. Near the close of 1962, the missile crisis terminated the migration, but by that time over 150,000 refugees had been admitted.

In 1965, the United States, through the Swiss Embassy in Havana, concluded a "memorandum of understanding" with Cuba providing for a regular monthly airlift of about 4,000 refugees from Cuba to the United States. This number of refugees could reasonably be processed

[14]Oscar Handlin, *The Newcomers: Negroes and Puerto Ricans in a Changing Metropolis* (Garden City, N.Y.: Doubleday 1962) pp. 50–54, 142.

[15]Richard R. Fagen, Richard A. Brody, and Thomas J. O'Leary, *Cubans in Exile: Disaffection and the Revolution* (Stanford, Ca.: Stanford Univ. Press, 1968), pp. 4–90.

each month. They were given proper attention as they arrived in Miami, Florida, the port of entry, and then were settled in Miami or elsewhere. By the end of 1966, an estimated 266,000 Cuban refugees were in the United States.

In selecting refugees for entry to the United States, priority went to immediate relatives of Cubans already in the United States: parents, spouses, unmarried children under twenty-one, and brothers and sisters under twenty-one. The refugees were classed as "parolees" rather than as permanent residents, under Section 212(d) (5) of the Immigration and Nationality Act.[16]

Although early refugees from Cuba may have had some funds, most migrants were stripped of their possessions by Cuban law, and they arrived in the United States without money. Since their parolee status is complex and no local or state welfare funds were available, the federal government had to supply necessary funds. Such public assistance monies are limited to providing needed assistance to refugees in the Miami area and to cover the costs of resettling refugees outside the Miami metropolitan area throughout the United States.

The center of the Cuban community in the United States is in Miami. Communications with refugees in other cities are maintained through both government and social contacts. Resettled Cubans, however, tend to blend into the general population of their new community, despite some language problems and a darker skin color than most of the general community. In Miami, though, they moved into the available low-cost housing and failed to integrate into the general community.

Since both Key West and Tampa have had colonies of Cubans for more than one hundred years, the presence of Cubans in Florida is not new. Miami has long had a substantial number of nationals from Cuba and other Latin American countries. Prior to the refugee migration of 1958 to 1967, there were about 20,000 Cubans living in the Miami area.

The characteristics of the migrating refugee population in the two major periods of migration (1958–1962; 1965–1967) have varied. The early population included a large proportion of professionals: lawyers, doctors, teachers, and government workers. Also, in the early population many unaccompanied women and children were sent to the care of friends, relatives, or the Catholic church. The later population contained more blue-collar workers, fishermen, and others in modest circumstances. The occupational distribution has remained heavily

---

[16] *Cuban Refugee Problems: Hearings Before the Subcommittee to Investigate Problems Connected with Refugees and Escapees of the Committee of the Judiciary, U.S. Senate, Eighty-Ninth Congress, Part I* (Washington, D.C.: U.S. Government Printing Office, 1966), p. 26.

weighted by the professional, managerial, and white-collar categories. The migration contained a disproportionately large number of females because the Castro government prohibited men of military age, defined as fifteen through twenty-six years of age, from leaving Cuba.

Perhaps the most striking characteristic of the population of Cuban refugees is the general high level of education. For example, the proportion who have completed four or more years of college is higher than that of the population in Dade County which, in turn, is higher than that of the United States in general.[17]

The refugees almost unanimously think they have been well treated in the United States by both public officials and the people of Miami. Although a great many, especially the elderly, have not acquired command of the English language, Cubans are becoming a culturally integrated element in Miami as a result of acculturation and diffusion.

Three categories of activities have been significant in controlling this migration for the benefit of the refugees as well as the non-Cuban population of Miami: (1) welfare and health services to the refugees; (2) resettlement of refugees to other areas of the country; and (3) training by the federal government, the community, and the refugees themselves to make all refugees self-sufficient.

Despite the problems anticipated by law enforcement officials, primarily because of crowding Cuban refugees into low-rent housing districts and the impoverished conditions of most refugees, the record of arrests of Cubans in Miami is very low. The average rate of arrests per hundred people over a period of three and a half years was much lower for Cubans than for other major racial or ethnic groups in Miami. Cuban women have even a better record, and arrests among Cuban juveniles have also been at a considerably lower rate than among other juveniles in this area.[18]

The Cuban refugees are no longer simply transitory visitors awaiting a favorable opportunity to return to Cuba. On the whole, they seem to be losing conviction that a change in Cuban circumstances will make return feasible. Although most refugees still hope to return, even if they do not regain their pre-Castro property or status, many are accumulating vested interests in the United States. An exodus of these migrants should political change occur in Cuba seems exceedingly remote, and more Cubans are working toward legal immigration to the United States.

[17] *The Cuban Immigration 1959–1966 and Its Impact on Dade County, Florida* (Coral Gables, Fla.: Center for Advanced Studies, Univ. of Miami, 1967), p. xii.

[18] *The Cuban Immigration*, p. xix.

BLACKS

Blacks in America are the largest and most visible minority. In 1900, blacks comprised about twelve percent of the total population; during the Irish, German, and Italian immigration periods, it dropped to ten percent; and in 1970 it was about eleven percent. In 1890, census data revealed a population of 7.5 million blacks; in 1910 it was 9.8 million; in 1930 blacks numbered 11.9 million; in 1950 the total black population was 15 million; and in 1970 it was close to 23 million.[19]

Human relationships shape criminal law and criminal justice procedures; but a study of American legal history shows that the founding fathers did not intend to include black men in the American body politic. The writers of the United States Constitution reduced blacks to the level of chattel. In the famous case of *Dred Scott* v. *Sanford*,[20] the Supreme Court ruled that blacks could not be considered citizens either by naturalization or by birthright.

This notorious court decision was oriented politically toward slaveholders and slave states. The description of slaves as mere property, forever denied citizenship and participation in government, inflamed the antislavery groups who believed in human and political rights for all and the nation moved toward civil war over the slavery issue.

The Emancipation Proclamation issued by President Lincoln and the subsequent passage of the Thirteenth and Fourteenth Amendments to the Constitution, seemed to indicate that the former slave was now a free man. Under the provisions of the Fourteenth Amendment, the states were forbidden to take life, liberty, or property without due process of law, or to deny anyone equal protection of the laws.

The *Slaughter-House Cases*[21] were the first cases brought under the Fourteenth Amendment, and they arose because the Louisiana state government had granted a monopoly of the slaughterhouse business to one concern, and thus prevented over one thousand other persons, including many blacks, and many firms from continuing their business. The case was argued before the Supreme Court twice and was decided in favor of the monopoly by a majority of five to four.

The three cases are reported under their common name, the *Slaughter-House Cases.* This action arose from an act of the Louisiana state legislature which was "to protect the health of the City of New Orleans, to locate the stock landings and slaughterhouses, and to incor-

[19] *Black Americans* (Washington, D.C.: Department of Labor, 1969), p. 4.
[20] 19 (Howard) U.S. 393 (1856).
[21] 16 (Wallace) U.S. 36 (1873).

porate 'The Crescent City Live-Stock Landing and Slaughter-House Company,'" which was approved on March 8, 1869, and went into operation on June 1; the three cases were argued together. The act granted to a private corporation the exclusive right for twenty-five years to slaughter cattle in an area of 150 square miles in and around New Orleans.

Hundreds of suits were brought on both sides; the butchers not included in the monopoly acted singly, in combinations, in corporations, and in companies; the same counsel, however, apparently represented all parties. The opposition to the slaughterhouse monopoly said that the act of the Louisiana legislature created a monopoly and violated the most important provisions of the Thirteenth and Fourteenth Amendments:

Amendment XIII.

Neither slavery nor *involuntary servitude* except as a punishment for crime, whereof the party shall have been duly convicted, shall exist within the United States, nor any place subject to their jurisdiction.

Amendment XIV.

All persons born or naturalized in the United States, and subject to the jurisdiction thereof, *are citizens of the United States* and of the State wherein they reside.

No State shall make or enforce any law which shall abridge the *privileges or immunities of citizens of the United States,* nor shall any State deprive any person of life, *liberty, or property,* without due process of law, nor deny to any person within its jurisdiction the *equal protection of the laws.*

The Louisiana Supreme Court decided in favor of the company, and five of the cases came into the United States Supreme Court. The decision of the U.S. Supreme Court affirmed the action of the state supreme court in favor of the monopoly, the Crescent City Live-Stock Landing and Slaughter-House Company. By its action in the *Slaughter-House Cases,* the Supreme Court failed to support the purpose of the Fourteenth Amendment regarding equal right to work.

The case for equal opportunity was set forth in Justice Field's dissenting opinion in this case. Extracts from this opinion are:

In all these cases there is a recognition of the equality of right among citizens in the pursuit of the ordinary avocations of life, and a declaration that all grants of exclusive privileges, in contravention of this equality, are against common right, and void.

This equality of right, with exemption from all disparaging and partial enactments, in the lawful pursuits of life, throughout the whole country, is the distinguishing privilege of citizens of the United States. To them, everywhere, all pursuits, all professions, all avocations are open without other restrictions than such as are imposed equally upon all others of the same age, sex, and condition. The State may prescribe such regulations for every pursuit and calling of life as will promote the public health, secure the good order and advance the general prosperity of society, but when once prescribed, the pursuit or calling must be free to be followed by every citizen who is within the conditions designated, and will conform to the regulations.

How widely this equality of right has been departed from, how entirely rejected and trampled upon by the act of Louisiana, I have already shown. And it is to me a matter of profound regret that its validity is recognized by a majority of this court, for by it the right of free labor, one of the most sacred and imprescriptible rights of man, is violated.

Grants of exclusive privileges, such as is made by the act in question, are opposed to the theory of free government, and it requires no aid from any Bill of Rights to render them void. That only is a free government, in the American sense of the term, under which the inalienable right of every citizen to pursue his happiness is unrestrained, except by just, equal and impartial laws.

The lawmakers of the federal government who had supported the antislave movement through the Civil War years and the Reconstruction labored diligently on the explicit language of the Civil War Amendments. The 1873 decision of the Supreme Court in the *Slaughter-House Cases* contradicted the legislative intent to prevent racial discrimination, and the judicial double-talk in the majority opinion over who were citizens and whether United States or state citizenship protected the basic right to work was an insult. In 1875 the U.S. Congress passed the Civil Rights Act to use federal power to prevent racial discrimination. The new law would affect all states, but it was aimed at the former slave-holding states, now governed primarily by whites, many of whom had fought on the side of the Confederacy in the Civil War. The Civil Rights Act of 1875 provided (in Section 1):

That all persons within the jurisdiction of the United States shall be entitled to the full and equal enjoyment of the accommodations, advantages, facilities, and privileges of inns, public conveyances on land and water, theatres, and other places of public amusement; subject only to the conditions and limitations established by law, and applicable alike to citizens of every race and color, regardless of any previous condition of servitude.[22]

[22] *Civil Rights Cases,* 109 U.S. 3 (1883), p. 9.

Section 2 of this act placed a penalty of $500 on violations of it (payable to the aggrieved person) and classed such violations as misdemeanors punishable upon conviction by a fine of $500 to $1,000, or thirty days to one year imprisonment.

In all, five lower court cases involving violations of this act were reviewed by the United States Supreme Court in 1883. They are known collectively as the "Civil Rights Cases." The defendants were Stanley, Nichols, Ryan, Singleton, and Robinson.

The cases against Stanley and Nichols are indictments for denying persons of color the accommodations and privileges of an inn or hotel. Those against Ryan and Singleton are for denying individuals the privileges and accommodations of a theater. The information against Ryan concerned refusing a seat in the dress circle of Maguire's Theater in San Francisco to a black, and the indictment against Singleton was for denying a person, of unstated color, the full enjoyment of the accommodations of the theater known as the Grand Opera House in New York. The case of Robinson and wife against the Memphis and Charleston Railroad Company concerned the conductors refusal to allow Robinson's wife to ride in the ladies' car because she was of African descent.

The Court's holding in the Civil Rights Cases was that the Civil Rights Act of 1857 was unconstitutional: Congress was not empowered by the Fourteenth Amendment to prevent or penalize racial discrimination by private individuals. Judicial review and authority in the United States had thus interpreted the wording of the Fourteenth Amendment in a manner which nullified the main thrust of the antislavery movement and the Civil War, the freeing of the black slaves. The war may have been directed against preventing the secession of the slave-holding states from the Union, but it was also fought over the issue of slavery. As the enactment of the three Civil War Amendments and the 1857 Civil Rights Act indicated, once free, blacks should receive equal treatment under law.

Racial segregation by private action after the decision in the Civil Rights Cases in 1883 was left to individual states. When the law required segregation, however, the question arose whether such laws violated the rights guaranteed by the Fourteenth Amendment.

In *Plessy* v. *Ferguson*,[23] the petitioner claimed to be seven-eights Caucasian and one-eighth African, that the mixture of "color" was not discernible in him, and that he was entitled to every right, privilege and immunity of white United States citizens. Acting on that theory, he took a vacant seat in the white section of a railroad car in Louisiana. The passenger was subsequently arrested under the state law calling for

[23]163 U.S. 537 (1896).

separate railway carriages or compartments for white and black races. This law also empowered employees of the railroads to assign a coach or compartment on the basis of race, and provided for a fine and incarceration should the provisions of the act not be carried out.

The case *Plessy* v. *Ferguson* made lawful for over fifty years the doctrine that black Americans could be denied equal protection of the laws by compelling racial segregation and forcing blacks to accept separate accommodations. Citizenship, due process and equal protection of the law, and the right to vote which had been guaranteed for the black minority as constitutional law under the Fourteenth and Fifteenth Amendments were delayed for over a hundred years, and during this time blacks were subjected to second-class citizenship under the Jim Crow laws of Southern States. Apparently the end of slavery was not the end of white supremacy in the former slave states.

The Jim Crow laws regulated every dimension of social contact between blacks and whites. Separate building entrances and exits, seating arrangements in theatres (or separate theatres), public transportation, waiting rooms in railroad stations (and later, separate bus stations and airports), toilets, drinking fountains, hotels, restaurants, and other accommodations were required for blacks.

The blacks that fled the South and traveled to cities in the North and Midwest may have escaped the formal social segregation of Jim Crow laws, but they encountered the de facto segregation in the North. Residential segregation in ghettos created segregated local schools which served the local neighborhoods. Lack of preparation for skilled jobs and limited education forced the blacks into menial, low-paying occupations. This complex of ghetto living and thwarted goals kept the black northerner in as much poverty as the black southerner. In the North, however, a black could vote, fewer law enforcement officers were white supremacists, and mob violence was isolated and sporadic.

From 1910 to 1950 there was a discernible shift of blacks from rural to urban areas. In 1910, 2.7 million blacks lived in cities, while 7.1 million lived in rural areas; in 1950, the urban black dwellers numbered 9.4 million, and the rural black residents were down to 5.6 million. The migration of blacks northward caused an explosion in the ratio of blacks to whites in many metropolitan areas. New York's black population represented 14 percent of the city's total population in 1950; in Chicago the 1960 black percentage of the city's population was 22.9 percent; and in Detroit, Philadelphia, and Washington, D.C., 1960 black population percentages of the total populations were 28.9, 26.4, and 53.9 respectively.

Although the black minority in the United States is on the threshold of its legal rights and has adopted a more militant posture of protest regarding racial prejudice and discrimination, most blacks still live in urban ghettos.

Failure of black youths to succeed in competition among youths, or to obtain a decent wage from prosperous businessmen intent only on maximizing their profits led to the following conclusion of an articulate New York black tired of long hours and low pay: "The only way to get real money from him [an employer] is to get a gun, go down there and put it to that mother-fucker's head and take it."[24]

DISCUSSION QUESTIONS

1. Discuss the concept of a disadvantaged minority. Is the rationale for this concept justified?
2. Trace the transition of the American Indian to minority status. Was this transition caused mainly by land frauds, by force, by "treaties," or by failure to make Indians citizens of the United States?
3. Describe the impact of Mexican agricultural labor (braceros, wetbacks, commuters) on the socioeconomic levels of the Mexican American residents of the Southwest.
4. What are the similarities and differences between the Mexican Americans and the Puerto Rican migrants? between the Mexican Americans and black Americans? between black and Cuban refugees?
5. What decisions of the United States Supreme Court nullified the Fourteenth Amendment's guarantee of equality to blacks?

CASE REFERENCES

Cherokee Nation v. *Georgia,* 30 U.S. (Peters 5) 1 (1831).

Civil Rights Cases, 109 U.S. 3 (1883).

Dred Scott v. *Sanford,* 19 (Howard) U.S. 393 (1856).

Plessy v. *Ferguson,* 163 U.S. 537 (1896).

Slaughter-House Cases, 16 (Wallace) U.S. 36 (1873).

[24]Claude Brown, *Manchild in the Promised Land* (New York: Macmillan, 1965), p. 284.

3

The Struggle
for
Civil Rights

SOCIAL-JUDICIAL MOVEMENT—NAACP
MILITANT CIVIL RIGHTS GROUPS
CULTURAL NATIONALISTS
REVOLUTIONARY NATIONALISTS
THE DEATH OF JIM CROW
NONSEGREGATED PUBLIC TRANSPORTATION
THE *BROWN* v. *BOARD OF EDUCATION* DECISION OF 1954
THE CIVIL RIGHTS ACT OF 1964

Although blacks and whites have fraternized on all levels, their relationships have been threatened frequently when the blacks involved sought equal status with whites. In the South, subordination of blacks was particularly overt in the Jim Crow laws and segregation in public education. In the North it was covert to some extent; residential segregation and de facto school segregation are fairly apparent, but racial discrimination is carefully guarded in trade unions.

The struggle for civil rights for all American minorities has been led by the most oppressed American minority, the blacks. Black leaders have fought to make the Thirteenth, Fourteenth, and Fifteenth Amendments a reality. On the one hand, the struggle has been a sophisticated, tactically well organized attack carried out in the courts of the

United States; on the other hand, it has been a spontaneous, unstructured attack on visible segregation. This attack took place in buses, restaurants, lunch counters, and schools; it was a legal, in-the-streets attack on the *Plessy* v. *Ferguson* doctrine of separate-but-equal facilities.

The concept of civil rights demonstrations and civil disobedience is virtually ageless. It has been traced back as far as the sixth century B.C., and elements of protest encompassing religious, political, and philosophical doctrine are contained in the Christian teachings of our modern churches. The founders of the United States rebelled against English rule by protest demonstrations and civil disobedience. Mahatma Gandhi used these techniques extensively in India in the early part of this century. Martin Luther King, Jr. developed civil disobedience into a highly effective means of coercive pressure for social change.

There is a tendency for law and order proponents and many law enforcement officials to view all forms of protest as civil disobedience with no attempt to distinguish between their methods. Such conclusions, without any analysis of the philosophies involved, link all black protest organizations and movements together into one group with the same ideology, philosophy, and intent. Various black protest groups, however, have different and changing philosophies and methods. These orientations range from nonviolent demonstrations to violent civil protest; and their goals range from integration to complete separation of blacks and whites.

The social-judicial group struggled to gain equality for blacks within the existing social order by enlisting the help of whites in the dominant group; the militant civil rights group sought the same goals by demonstrations and freedom rides. Black nationalists believe in separation from white America and its white society, whereas the revolutionary nationalists have espoused nothing less than an equality likely to result in overthrowing the capitalist system and establishing a socialist democracy. The social-judicial group seeks integration by nonviolent means; the cultural nationalists reject integration; and the revolutionary nationalists seek integration by any means, usually violence, and advocate absolute equality.

SOCIAL-JUDICIAL MOVEMENT—NAACP

The period from 1905 to 1955 is significant for the social-judicial movement. W. E. B. DuBois, the eminent black scholar, organized the Niagara Movement, forerunner of the National Association for the

Advancement of Colored People (NAACP); and in 1910, the National Urban League was founded as a social work agency to deal with the problems of cities and southern black migrants. These organizations forced some progress; the NAACP pioneered in appealing cases of unequal treatment to the U.S. Supreme Court and used the judicial process to force executive and legislative action.

William Edward Burghardt DuBois was an educator and intellectual who stressed education for blacks in the liberal arts rather than in vocational training. He was born in Massachusetts in 1868, and his early brilliance as a scholar earned him scholarships at Harvard and the University of Berlin, acceptance as a Rhodes scholar at Oxford, and a faculty appointment at Howard University. DuBois was uncompromising in his view that the black minority was entitled to develop fully all of its faculties and talents and that the accident of black birth should not serve as a limitation.[1]

The National Association for the Advancement of Colored People (NAACP) was formed in 1910, and it soon became the dominant force in black protests against segregation, denial of suffrage, and inadequate education. DuBois was a leader in the NAACP who merged his Niagara Movement with it and served as articulate spokesman in later years. Thurgood Marshall was chief legal counsel for the NAACP and earned his nickname "Mister Civil Rights" in twenty-four years of legal one-upmanship in attacking the antiblack activity in America. His native state was Maryland, he was educated in law at Howard University, and he practiced law in Baltimore. In 1967 he was appointed to the U.S. Supreme Court by President Lyndon B. Johnson.

Guided by Marshall, the NAACP assisted in successfully managing most of the cases brought before appellate tribunals which established the rights of blacks to vote, to travel from state to state without the restrictions of Jim Crow laws, and to send their children to desegregated public schools. The 1954 decision of the U.S. Supreme Court abolishing the separate-but-equal concept in public education was a high point in the NAACP's fight for desegregation, and thus an important step toward improving the quality of black education.[2] The NAACP has been the leading organization in the social-judicial movement for black equality. A skilled legal and management staff, adequate financial reserves, prompt action in protecting the rights of the black minority, and professional assistance to blacks arrested during civil rights demonstrations helped to make the NAACP influential.

[1]Norval D. Glenn and Charles M. Bonjean, *Blacks in the United States* (San Francisco: Chandler, 1969), p. 329.

[2]*Brown* v. *Board of Education*, 347 U.S. 483 (1954).

The Urban League was organized in 1911. Its goals were limited: to help blacks adjust to city life. It dealt diplomatically with white leadership in urban politics and business. The Urban League's major contribution has been in social work, but it also contributed friends and finances to the NAACP to support the civil rights struggle.

MILITANT CIVIL RIGHTS GROUPS

The Congress of Racial Equality (CORE) was founded in 1942, the Southern Christian Leadership Conference (SCLC) was begun in 1957, and the Student Nonviolent Coordinating Committee (SNCC) was formed in 1960.

James Farmer, executive director of CORE, was a Methodist minister. He was born in Texas and earned a bachelor's degree in science before entering Howard University's School of Religion. CORE was the first black protest group organized around the theme of nonviolence and passive resistance advocated by Mahatma Gandhi. In 1950, CORE developed the *standing line* (persistent waiting in line) to harrass restaurants which refused to serve blacks. In 1961 CORE introduced the freedom ride, which sent groups of protestors on interstate buses to the South in a giant protest against separate-but-equal facilities. White anger at the freedom riders led to private and official violence against them and directed the nation's attention to the racial segregation in modern America.

Floyd Bixler McKissick replaced James Farmer as the head of CORE in 1966. McKissick was born in North Carolina in 1922, educated in North Carolina schools and colleges, and took his law degree at the University of North Carolina. For seventeen years he was an attorney in North Carolina specializing in constitutional law and pleading the cause of many blacks. Under McKissick's leadership CORE emphasized black power because he believed that black power was not antiwhite so much as it was pro-black, not a racist movement but a necessary development.[3]

The Southern Christian Leadership Conference is identified with the leadership of Dr. Martin Luther King. Dr. King was born in Atlanta, Georgia, to a family of ministers, and he graduated from Atlanta's Morehouse College, and Crozer Theological Seminary in Pennsylvania, and Boston University, earning B.A., D.D., and Ph.D. degrees. In Montgomery, Alabama, in 1955, the Reverend Martin Luther King and a devoted group of followers began a full-fledged struggle against Jim Crow prac-

---

[3]Floyd McKissick, *Three-Fifths of a Man*, (New York: MacMillan, 1969), p. 141.

tices with their protest over the seating of a black seamstress on a local bus. King and his followers decided to use nonviolent action in the spirit of Mahatma Gandhi. As the movement's leader, Dr. King fired the imaginations of blacks and activated black involvement throughout the United States and the world. Although his opponents often resorted to violent tactics, he continued to preach nonviolence and said that it was wrong and personally degrading to hate.

On Good Friday in 1963, Dr. King culminated the SCLC's nonviolent protests by leading a march of protestors to the center of Birmingham, where the police dispersed the group with dogs, clubs, and fire hoses. In 1965, Dr. King and other leaders of the SCLC led thousands of protestors from Selma, Alabama, to Montgomery, the state capital, to dramatize their opposition to the denial of voting rights to blacks in the Selma area. Again they were met with official violence, but this time it was so intemperate that President Lyndon B. Johnson stated publicly that he deplored such treatment of people having sincere interest in attaining the precious right to vote.

The context in which Dr. King gained prominence and worldwide support should be recalled. American blacks indentified increasingly with the rise of independent African states. In addition, the exposure of domestic racism in America threatened the position of the United States as leader of the "free" world. Some black governments in Africa had become independent of European colonial domination and exploitation. These Africans were now freed from total economic and political dependence on whites. Worldwide television coverage of the demonstrations organized by King's movement was also an essential factor in the movement's mass appeal.

There is little doubt that Dr. King's nonviolence and the official violent reaction in Alabama encouraged President John Kennedy to move beyond the moderate posture that had characterized his administration on racial issues and to propose a Civil Rights Bill to Congress in 1963. After President Kennedy's death, President Lyndon B. Johnson pressed Congress, and the Civil Rights Act of 1964 was passed.

The Student Nonviolent Coordinating Committee (SNCC) was a youth action group centered on college campuses and from its beginnings it was a dynamic militant group although pledged to nonviolence. It was a leading exponent of sit-ins to desegregate places which discriminated against blacks, and its members protested by refusing to pay fines, by serving jail sentences, and by participating in freedom rides, freedom schools, and jail-ins. Both Stokely Carmichael and H. Rap Brown were chairmen of this group before they became black nationalists.

CULTURAL NATIONALISTS

One early organization among blacks did not seek equality in the American community but a return to Africa: the Universal Negro Improvement Association (UNIA), organized in 1920, and led by Marcus Garvey. Garvey was born in the West Indies, was a printer early in life, and slipped into newspaper publishing just before founding the UNIA.

The promise of consumer cooperatives, a new church (the African Orthodox Church), parades, titles of nobility, and paramilitary units were all used by Garvey to stir the thoughts of black people whose hopes had been suppressed by slavery, oppression, and colonization. His was the first, the largest, and the most significant movement of its kind among black people in the United States.

Coming to New York City from Jamaica in 1916, Marcus Garvey found an audience among many Southern blacks who had come north to escape the oppressive conditions in the South. An orator of unusual talent, he recruited followers for his concept of black nationalism, started a newspaper (*The Negro World*), and went into the steamship business. In 1925, Garvey was sent to prison for using the United States mails to defraud in connection with the sale of stocks in his steamship company, the Black Star Line.[4] Following a two-year prison term he was deported to his native Jamaica and died in 1940. Marcus Garvey was a visionary destroyed by his inability to solve financial problems. He captivated the interest and respect of the ordinary black American as no other former leader had. He failed to understand, however, that the overwhelming mass of American blacks considered America their rightful home and had no real desire to leave it.

The beginnings of the present Nation of Islam, or the Black Muslims, can be traced to 1913, when a North Carolina black named Timothy Drew formed a Moorish Science Temple in Newark, New Jersey. Drew developed the idea that American blacks could achieve salvation simply by making themselves into Asiatics, or more specifically, *Moors*. Drew, now called Drew Ali, linked American blacks to the North African people. He did not tell his followers to leave the United States; his "emigration" was purely psychological. He died in 1929, but the movement did not terminate upon his death.

In 1930, a person appeared who claimed he was the reincarnation of Drew Ali. He was a light-skinned black, of Oriental mien, named W. D. Fard. He appeared in Detroit's black ghetto as a peddler of silks and

[4]There are some overtones of a political trial; the prosecutor may have been intent on "beheading" the UNIA by destroying its leader.

soon became the leader of a small cult of Moors with headquarters in a Temple of Islam. By 1933, he was reputed to have eight thousand followers, some who believed he was the reincarnation of Drew Ali, others who believed he was God. Fard disappeared from Detroit in the summer of 1933 or 1934.

A splinter group from the Detroit temple during Fard's leadership founded a similar cult in Chicago. Its leader was Elijah Muhammad, born Elijab Poole in Sandersville, Georgia, in 1897. Elijah Muhammad, who claims to be infallible, believes that Fard now resides in Mecca and will live until he is 444 years old.

Black Muslims are followers of Elijah Muhammad, Spiritual Leader of the Lost-Found Nation in the West. Black Muslims are not orthodox Moslems because they believe that Elijah Muhammad is the Messenger of Allah, directly commissioned by Allah to wake up the sleeping black nation and rid them of the white man's lengthy domination.[5] The Black Muslims are basically a religious movement but are also a protest group. They fight white racism which has blocked the black man's progress since the emancipation of the slaves. Black Muslims believe that the black man must develop skills and resources and that all blacks must pool their resources for the common good of a strong and prosperous nation under Allah.

Black Muslims emphasize economic separation, and the theme of black capitalism has led to a strong financial base for their nation. Funds come from taxes on members; sale of *Muhammad Speaks,* the Muslim newspaper; and profits from several million dollars invested in various Muslim enterprises.

A Muslim must not drink, smoke, swear, lie, steal, gossip, or gamble. He must not commit adultery, use skin bleaches, or show disrespect to his ministers. He must maintain a high standard of personal hygiene, dress conservatively, keep his home tidy, pray five times a day, and eat only one daily meal. He must not vote in elections, salute the American flag, or join the military forces of the United States.

Malcolm X was Muhammad's right-hand man in the Black Muslims until he resigned in 1963 and founded the Organization of African Unity (OAU). He was born Malcolm Little in Omaha, Nebraska, in 1925. He lost his parents early in life, and dropped out of school in eighth grade. While in a New York prison, he was converted to the views of Muhammad, and became an advocate of self-help, self-defense, and education as a route to upward mobility. He was assassinated in 1965

[5]C. Eric Lincoln, *The Black Muslims in America* (Boston, Mass.: Beacon Press, 1961), p. 21.

after being suspended from the Black Muslim movement. At the time of his death he had changed from a cultural nationalist (Black Muslim) to a position aligned with the revolutionary nationalists (Black Panthers).

REVOLUTIONARY NATIONALISTS

The Black Panthers were formally organized in 1966, by two blacks under thirty: Huey Newton and Bobby Seale. Newton's and Seale's parents moved their families to the California Bay Area (San Francisco and Oakland) where both young men were educated in California's public schools. Although both attended classes to the junior college level, Newton claims he was illiterate when he graduated from high school.[6]

The Black Panthers draw members from the disenchanted and disadvantaged blacks of the ghetto. As revolutionary nationalists they stress the right to self-defense, hold the basic assumption that the black minority in America is a colonized people in colonial bondage, and believe that violence against the police and other white agents is not criminal but revolutionary.

Eldridge Cleaver, noted black writer and an early supporter and member of the Black Panthers, reports that Huey Newton described the goals of the organization:

> Our message is one and the same. We're going to talk about black people arming themselves in a political fashion to exert organized force in the political arena to see to it that their desires and needs are met. Otherwise there will be a political consequence. And the only culture worth talking about is a revolutionary culture. So it doesn't matter what heading you put on it, we're going to talk about political power growing out of the barrel of a gun.[7]

Black revolutionary nationalists, such as Malcolm X, Huey Newton, Bobby Seale, and Eldridge Cleaver, think that the black community should sever all relations with white society. This separatist theme no doubt stems from the recognition that blacks were already separated from an "establishment" which refused to grant them power. This exclusion from any political, social, or economic power and rewards led

[6]Huey Newton, *Revolutionary Suicide* (New York: Harcourt Brace Jovanovich, 1973), p. 53.

[7]Robert Scheer, ed., *Eldridge Cleaver: Post-prison Writings and Speeches* (New York: Random House, 1969), p. 31.

to frustration and bitterness, and blacks decided to seek alternative paths to success by complete separation from whites.

The strategy of revolutionary black nationalists in developing parallel black organizations to established white institutions is to define black identity and unite black people for political action. Local military defense of a black neighborhood is the prime illustration of such organized black power. The Black Panthers (or a local organization such as the Blackstone Rangers in Chicago) serve to some extent as a local militia. They organize paramilitary training and purchase weapons, and conflict often arises between this neighborhood force and police representing the central government.

Direct combat is of little value to the local groups because the central police force is much more powerful. Shoot-outs between Black Panthers and police have been violent and costly. On the other hand, political defense of local rights can be valuable but requires the general education of blacks at local levels (such as SNCC's freedom schools and the Freedom Democratic Party throughout Mississippi) to gain their loyalty and to prevent internal division and subversion of local residents.[8]

THE DEATH OF JIM CROW

As presently organized, the cultural nationalists (Black Muslims) and revolutionary nationalists (Black Panthers) did not contribute a great deal to the civil rights struggle. The work of the social-judicial groups, primarily the NAACP, and the nonviolent crusades of Dr. King and the SCLC forced the enactment of the 1964 Civil Rights Act and contributed to the U.S. Supreme Court decisions which finally put blacks in a position to receive the equal protection of the law.

The term *Jim Crow* comes from a line in a Negro song, "Wheel about and turn about and jump Jim Crow." It was popularized by T. D. Rice, a well-known black song-and-dance man in about 1835 and has become an effective term for describing laws subordinating blacks to whites. Jim Crow symbolizes a method of oppression to the black man and forces him to remember his low status and to humble himself to whites through fear of arrest or violence. Because of Jim Crow, men staged sit-ins and jail-ins, marches and freedom rides to demonstrate that blacks should not be given separate-but-equal treatment. It was almost a century before Jim Crow met his death.

[8]Milton Kotler, *Neighborhood Government: The Local Foundations of Political Life* (New York: Bobbs-Merrill, 1969), pp. 58–59, 89–93.

NONSEGREGATED PUBLIC TRANSPORTATION

Decisions of the United States Supreme Court were responsible for the passing away of *Jim Crow* in its most visible form, public transportation. In 1962 the Court stated, "We have settled beyond question that no State may require racial segregation of interstate or intrastate transportation facilities. . . . The question is no longer open; it is foreclosed as a litigable issue."[9]

Morgan v. *Virginia*[10] was an appeal of the state court conviction of an interstate passenger for conduct which violated Virginia state law requiring the segregation of white and "colored" passengers on motor buses. The appeal to the Supreme Court raised the question of the law's constitutionality. The appeal attacked the Virginia law on the grounds that it imposed undue burdens on interstate commerce, but the opposition (government of Virginia) claimed the law was enacted and enforced in the exercise of the state's police power to avoid friction between the races. The Court, however, had pointed out years ago "that a State cannot avoid this rule [undue burdens on interstate commerce] by simply invoking the convenient apologetics of the police power."[11]

The Court's holding in *Morgan* was that the Virginia law was invalid:

> As there is no federal act dealing with the separation of races in interstate transportation, we must decide the validity of this Virginia statute on the challenge that it interferes with commerce, as a matter of balance between the exercise of the local police power and the need for national uniformity in the regulations for interstate travel. It seems clear to us that seating arrangements for the different races in interstate motor travel require a single, uniform rule to promote and protect national travel. Consequently, we hold the Virginia statute in controversy invalid.[12]

In 1960, the U.S. Supreme Court reaffirmed the doctrine of *Morgan* and foreshadowed the Court's action in holding the 1964 Civil Rights Act as constitutional under the Commerce Clause rather than under the authority of the Fourteenth Amendment. This 1960 case was *Boynton* v. *Virginia*,[13] and it came to the Court on an appeal from a conviction of Boynton, a black law student who was a passenger en

[9]*Bailey* v. *Patterson*, 369 U.S. 31 (1962), p. 33.

[10]328 U.S. 373 (1946).

[11]*Kansas City Southern R.R. Company* v. *Kaw Valley*, 233 U.S. 75 (1913), p. 79.

[12]*Morgan* v. *Virginia*, 328 U.S. 373 (1946), p. 386.

[13]364 U.S. 454 (1960).

route from Washington, D.C., to Montgomery, Alabama, on a Trailways bus. Boynton was convicted of a misdemeanor trespass under Virginia law for entering and refusing to leave a section of the Richmond, Virginia, bus terminal restaurant reserved for white people.

The basic question presented in *Boynton* was whether an interstate bus passenger is denied a federal statutory or constitutional right when a restaurant in a bus terminal used by the carrier along its route discriminates in serving food to the passenger solely because of his color. The Court's holding in *Boynton* was that Boynton, as a paying bus passenger, had a right to eat and to expect food to be available on his journey, and that it would be provided for him and for other passengers without discrimination prohibited by the Interstate Commerce Act.

THE *BROWN* v. *BOARD OF EDUCATION* DECISION OF 1954

The landmark decision of *Brown* v. *Board of Education*[14] arose from conditions in Kansas, South Carolina, Virginia, and Delaware. Although there were different facts and locales, there was one common factor: the aid of the court was sought to obtain the admission of black students to public schools on a nonsegregated basis. All of the plaintiffs—parents and children—had been injured in that they had applied and were denied admission to schools attended by white children because of state laws requiring or permitting racial segregation. They had also been denied relief in state courts under the separate-but-equal doctrine enunciated in *Plessy* v. *Ferguson*.[15] In arriving at the *Brown* decision, the Supreme Court viewed the problem as more than a question of whether or not black schools were equal to white schools. They stated it was now vital to view the problem as the effect of segregation itself on public education.

In *Brown* the United States Supreme Court admitted lack of available psychological data to the Court in 1896 when *Plessy* v. *Ferguson* was reviewed, and rejected the *Plessy* decision, holding that since that time modern reports had found that segregation of white and black children has a detrimental effect upon blacks. The segregation policy is usually interpreted by blacks as denoting their inferiority, and this sense of inferiority affects the motivation of a child to learn. The 1954 court summarized their decision in *Brown:*

[14]347 U.S. 483 (1954).
[15]163 U.S. 537 (1896).

We conclude that in the field of public education the doctrine of "separate-but-equal" has no place. Separate education facilities are inherently unequal. Therefore, we hold that the plaintiffs and others similarly situated for whom the actions have been brought are, by reason of the segregation complained of, deprived of the equal protection of the laws guaranteed by the Fourteenth Amendment.[16]

The decision in *Brown* outlawed discrimination based purely on race in public educational institutions. The opinion of the Court is grounded in the sound notion that a good education is an essential element of a democratic society and a requisite to the most basic public responsibilities.

Desegregation of public education did not proceed, however, with all deliberate speed. As late as 1973, almost two decades after *Brown*, some southern states were still operating "private" schools for white children, and the "desegregated" public schools were almost wholly attended by black children. In some northern cities there was de facto segregation because of the school's location in or near a black ghetto and because white parents refused to let their children be bussed in order to desegregate schools.

White Citizens' Councils and racial hatred surfaced in this struggle for equal protection under the laws and an effective education for blacks. County officials and school boards refused to appropriate funds for public schools in districts where white parents sent their children to "private" schools, and buses were damaged by dynamite and fire in schoolyards when bussing was used to desegregate de facto black schools.

This struggle over the doctrine and edict of *Brown* has placed America only on the threshold of desegregated public education. Judicial decrees can uphold the doctrine of *Brown*, but actual implementation needs political and community support, from the President to parents across the nation.

Again, sectionalism and local option often work against federal law. In some areas the concept of white supremacy has been retained, and dynamiters and arsonists of White Citizens' Councils and similar groups have acted out their hostility. Unfortunately, a generation of white and black children will always have some emotional scars from the appeal and rejection of black students since the 1954 *Brown* decision.

[16]*Brown* v. *Board of Education,* 347 U.S. 483 (1954), p. 495.

THE CIVIL RIGHTS ACT OF 1964

As early as 1866, Congress evidenced its interest in civil rights with its first Civil Rights or Enforcement Act of April 9, 1866. Four more acts (Slave Kidnapping Act; Peonage Abolition Act; Act of May 31, 1870; and the Anti-Lynching Act) followed this initial attempt to legislate equality, with a fifth law (Civil Rights Act of 1875) culminating the series. This 1875 act was declared unconstitutional in 1883 by the Supreme Court's decision in the Civil Rights Cases.[17] For eighty-two years after 1883, representatives of the central federal government abdicated any use of federal power to enforce the constitutional guarantees to equality as reaffirmed in the Civil War Amendments to the Constitution.

In 1957, a new series of civil rights laws was initiated in Congress. The Civil Rights Act of 1957 was followed by legislation of the same name in 1960 and 1964. The 1964 Civil Rights Act was a very comprehensive undertaking to prevent through peaceful and voluntary settlement discrimination in voting, places of accommodation and public facilities, federally-secured programs, and employment. It allows aggrieved persons to sue those who violate this legislation, permits the U.S. Attorney General to intervene on behalf of the plaintiff in such litigation, and establishes an administrative unit within the Department of Justice, to be known as the Community Relations Service, with the power to hold hearings and otherwise administrate this law.

The lead section, Section 201(a), of the 1964 Civil Rights Act provides that:

> All persons shall be entitled to the full and equal enjoyment of the goods, services, facilities, privileges, advantages, and accommodations of any place of public accommodation, as defined in this section, without discrimination or segregation on the ground of race, color, religion, or national origin.

Subdivision "b" lists the classes of business establishments covered.

Heart of Atlanta Motel v. *United States*[18] involved an action brought by a motel owner of Birmingham, Alabama, for a declaratory judgment as to the constitutionality of the public accommodations section of the Civil Rights Act of 1964 and for injunctive relief. Prior to passage of the act, the motel management maintained a policy of refusing to rent

[17]109 U.S. 3 (1883).
[18]379 U.S. 241 (1964).

rooms to blacks and stated openly that it continued to do so since enactment of this law. The contention of the motel management was that Congress, in passing the Civil Rights Act of 1964, had exceeded its power under Article I, Section 8, of the United States Constitution, and they claimed that:

> The Act violates the Fifth Amendment because appellant is deprived of the right to choose its customers and operate its business as it wishes, resulting in a taking of its liberty and property without due process of law and a taking of its property without just compensation and, finally, that by requiring appellant to rent available rooms to Negroes against its will, Congress is subjecting it to involuntary servitude in contravention of the Thirteenth Amendment.[19]

After a lengthy analysis, the U.S. Supreme Court held that Congress had the power to enact the Civil Rights Act of 1964 under the commerce clause as applied to a place of accommodation serving interstate travelers. This decision distinguished the case from the *Civil Rights Cases*[20] which struck down a similar law because its constitutional base was the Civil War Amendments. The Court used the meaning of the commerce clause, as first defined in 1824 by Chief Justice Marshall in *Gibbons* v. *Ogden.*[21]

Such Supreme Court support, under any section of the Constitution, was a giant step forward in overcoming racial discrimination. The Civil Rights Act of 1964 was the most far-reaching attack on race discrimination in America's history and contains the essence of many of the guarantees in the Fourteenth Amendment.

Mr. Justice Goldberg, in a concurring opinion in the foregoing case, pointed out that the Court could have rejected the 1883 doctrine of the Civil Rights Cases and held that Congress had the authority to enact the 1964 act under the Fourteenth Amendment as well as the commerce clause:

> Section 1 of the Fourteenth Amendment guarantees to all Americans the constitutional right to be treated as equal members of the community with respect to public accommodations and that Congress has authority under Section 5 of the Fourteenth Amendment, or under the Commerce Clause, Article I, Section 8, to implement the rights protected by Section 1 of the Fourteenth Amendment.[22]

[19]*Heart of Atlanta Motel* v. *U.S.,* 379 U.S. 241 (1964), pp. 243–44.
[20]109 U.S. 3 (1883).
[21]22 U.S. (Wheaton 9) 1 (1824).
[22]*Heart of Atlanta Motel* v. *United States,* p. 293.

Once the Supreme Court had held that Congress had the authority under the commerce clause of the Consitution to prohibit discrimination by hotels which received a substantial portion of their clientele from out of state, the next question facing the Court was whether the Civil Rights Act of 1964 applied to restaurant owners, or was limited to hotel owners. This question was also decided on the same day as the *Heart of Atlanta Motel* case, December 14, 1964.

The situation in *Katzenbach* v. *McClung*[23] involved a family business known as "Ollie's Barbecue" which catered to a family and white-collar trade with take-out service for blacks. A three-judge district court had found that a substantial portion of the food served in the restaurant had moved in interstate commerce. The court found also that if the restaurant were required to serve blacks it would lose a substantial amount of business, and it granted Ollie's (McClung) an injunction against government interference with its business operations.

The Supreme Court ruled in this case:

> Congress acted well within its power to protect and foster commerce in extending coverage of Title II, only to those restaurants offering to serve interstate travelers or serving food, a substantial portion of which moved in interstate commerce, since it had a rational basis to conclude that racial discrimination by such restaurants burdened interstate trade.[24]

This second case to uphold the 1964 Civil Rights Act was followed by another decision, on the same day, of the Supreme Court which also upheld the 1964 act.

The third case, *Hamm* v. *City of Rock Hill*,[25] developed because conduct against *Jim Crow* laws was no longer considered unlawful. The 1964 Civil Rights Act created a federal antidiscrimination law which, under the supremacy clause of the Consitution, must prevail against conflicting state Jim Crow laws. In *Hamm*, the petitioners were blacks convicted of state trespass laws for their behavior during sit-ins at lunch counters of retail stores. The Court found that, since the lunch counters had refused service to blacks, the sit-ins were a justified protest. Although the Civil Rights Act of 1964 was passed after the sit-ins and the convictions of the petitioners in state courts, the Supreme Court's decision was based on the 1964 act in accordance with an 1801 doctrine expressed by Chief Justice Marshall in *United States* v. *Schooner Peggy:*

[23]379 U.S. 294 (1964).
[24]*Katzenbach* v. *McClung*, p. 304.
[25]379 U.S. 306 (1964).

But if subsequent to the judgment and before the decision of the
appellate court, a law intervenes and positively changes the rule [old law]
which governs, the law [new] must be obeyed, or its obligation denied.
If the law be constitutional, I know of no court which can contest its
obligation.[26]

This trio of decisions by the United States Supreme Court indicated
that by December 14, 1964, members of the Court no longer believed
they alone articulated the principles of freedom and equality that can
make life meaningful for millions of people, black and white. In the
1954 *Brown* decision the Court order to desegregate public education
was virtually alone, but its leadership for equality under law led to the
1957, 1960, and 1964 Civil Rights Acts. The public began to notice that
Congress was dedicated to prohibiting racial discrimination, and the
Court's support of the 1964 act illustrated a renewed and sincere inten-
tion to deal honorably with the nation's black population.

The long and rigorous struggle for equality under law thus resulted
in some rewards for blacks. The Fourteenth Amendment became a
reality after many blacks had been arrested, jailed, indicted, and convicted for "loitering", "disturbing the peace," "trespassing", and violations of the *Jim Crow* state laws discriminating against blacks. Without
these protests, nothing would have changed, because only aggrieved
persons damaged by discriminatory laws can petition the appellate
courts for legal remedies.

In addition, public notice was directed toward the problem by the
behavior of these fearless and willing victims, aided by funds and the
legal talent of the NAACP and joined by the protest movement's mass
of demonstrators organized by groups such as the SNCC, and the SCLC.
By no other means could public concern and congressional representatives have been forced to focus on the basic injustice of racial discrimination and segregation on buses and trains, in schools, at lunch counters,
restaurants, hotels, and motels.

DISCUSSION QUESTIONS

1. What is the difference between black cultural nationalists and revolutionary nationalists?
2. What organization sparked the legal strategy and tactics of black protest
   for civil rights? What is the history of this organization?

[26]1 (Cranch) U.S. 103 (1801), p. 110.

3. What cases were decided in 1964 that indicated public policy in America had definitely swung away from racial discrimination?
4. Why were the Interstate Commerce Act and the commerce clause of the Constitution used to validate black civil rights instead of the Fourteenth Amendment?
5. What was the rationale for the United States Supreme Court's decision in *Brown* v. *Board of Education?*

CASE REFERENCES

Bailey v. *Patterson,* 369, U.S. 31 (1962).
Boynton v. *Virginia,* 364 U.S. 454 (1960).
Brown v. *Board of Education,* 347 U.S. 483 (1954).
Hamm v. *City of Rock Hill,* 379 U.S. 306 (1964).
Heart of Atlanta Motel v. *United States,* 379 U.S. 241 (1964).
Katzenbach v. *McClung,* 394 U.S. 279 (1964).
Morgan v. *Virginia,* 328 U.S. 373 (1946).
Plessy v. *Ferguson,* 163 U.S. 537 (1896).

4

Violent Confrontations

Emancipation of the slaves and subsequent enactment of amendments to the Constitution structuring this freedom in no way established the horizons of freedom. Although the separate-but-equal concept has been rejected, blacks have not yet been accepted on equal terms. The offspring of British colonists in America and the children of various eras of European immigrants who have become naturalized United States citizens are still conscious of color. Despite changes in law and social practice produced by the thrust of the civil rights movement, the great mass of blacks in America are unaffected, and people group together on

54

ghetto street corners to discuss black power or the ecstasy of long, hot summers. They are still hungry, unemployed, and hostile.[1]

The Civil War was a bloody, fratricidal conflict in which men fought for national agreement on the issue of slavery. Freedom and equality for the slaves were more than an ideal for which Union soldiers died; the birth and existence of the United States itself depended on making the concepts of liberty, freedom, and equality a meaningful reality for all citizens. Not all whites, however, can conquer their petty prejudices and think of the racial problem as involving these fundamental human rights.

Widespread fear of slave rebellion existed in the South before the Civil War, because slaves outnumbered their masters and often the total local white population. Rumors of plots and revolts and reports of slave unrest were common, as were reassurances minimizing the danger: the slaves were both unarmed and unaccustomed to using arms, and slave rebellions could be suppressed easily by local militia. Tales of slave conspiracies persisted because of the increasing insubordination of slaves and the growing number who fled to the North. These runaways were viewed as potential insurrectionists.

In 1831 a slave revolt in Virginia reinforced this fear. Nat Turner, born in 1800 and a lifetime resident of Virginia, was a slave who learned to read. His contemporaries respected his keen intellectual capacity. Turner led five slaves in revolt, killing his master and family, arming themselves, and stealing six horses. Within twenty-four hours, the news of Nat Turner's revolt spread among local slaves and his followers increased to about seventy. Turner led them on a twenty-mile march toward the county seat, where arms were stored, during which fifty to sixty whites were killed. Turner and his group battled white volunteers and local militia outside of town, but they were unable to overcome the armed defenders of the county seat. Federal troops and Virginia militia soon entered the area and hunted down Turner's followers. Many were killed during the roundup; survivors were promptly tried and executed. Turner went into hiding, but was discovered in a few weeks, pled not guilty at trial, was convicted, sentenced to death, and executed.[2]

OFFICIAL VIOLENCE

Official violence is best defined as the use of physical force by police and other agents of government. If justified, the use of violence is necessary

---

[1]C. Eric Lincoln, "Color and Group Identity in the United States," *Daedalus* (Journal of the American Academy of Arts and Sciences), Vol. 96, No. 2, Spring 1967, pp. 527–41.

[2]Herbert Aptheker, *American Negro Slave Revolts* (New York: International Publishers, 1943), pp. 18–19, 36.

and lawful; if "approved," the use of force has the approval of police associates (and sometimes community acceptance), and the behavior is not usually penalized by applying legal sanctions; if unjustified and unlawful, there is little doubt that the violence is criminal. The legality of official violence is often a matter of judgment by prosecutor, grand jury, and the judiciary.

This definition of official violence assumes that police brutality involves physical force but does not describe the language and manner of the police involved. Verbal abuse no doubt leads to physical violence and is a just area of complaint about police behavior, but it is not official violence.

Official violence has traditionally been caused by private violence, but the administration of Franklin D. Roosevelt responded to the private violence of labor in disputes with management for better wages and working conditions without resorting to violent tactics. The official reaction to "race riots" before the 1960s was a benign form of official violence directed at the whites who were terrorizing black ghettos. Color-conscious official violence places the police in a white supremist role; this official violence fails to curtail protests and often contributes to its spread and increased intensity.

All lawful governments have a right to use official violence to prevent anarchy or the overthrow of government by force and violence so that domestic tranquility will be preserved and government will be changed by a participatory political process open to all citizens, rather than by violence and the use of arms. Color-conscious official violence, however, is criminal and unjustified. It is the modern counterpart of frontier vigilantism or southern lynching by police seeking to destroy black leadership by overreacting in suppressing disorders.

The case of *United States* v. *Price*[3] is a classic case of color-conscious official violence. On June 21, 1964, Cecil Ray Price, Deputy Sheriff of Neshoba County, Mississippi, detained Michael Henry Schwerner, James Earl Chaney, and Andrew Goodman (three SNCC freedom workers) in the county jail located in Philadelphia, Mississippi. He released them in the dark of that night. He then proceeded by automobile on Highway 19 to intercept his erstwhile wards. He removed the three men from their automobile, placed them in an official automobile of the Neshoba County sheriff's office, and transported them to a place on an unpaved road.

It was alleged that these acts were part of a plan whereby the three men were intercepted by the eighteen defendants, including Deputy Sheriff Price, Sheriff Rainey, and Patrolman Willis of the Philadelphia

[3]383 U.S. 787 (1966).

Police Department. The purpose of the release from custody and the interception, according to the charge, was to "punish" the three men. The defendants, it is alleged, "did willfully assault, shoot, and kill" each of the three. And, the charge continues, the bodies of the three victims were transported by one of the defendants from the rendezvous on the unpaved road to the vicinity of the construction site of an earthen dam approximately five miles southwest of Philadelphia, Mississippi.

In this case two indictments were returned in the United States District Court for the Southern District of Mississippi against the defendants, police officers, and private individuals, charging them with two criminal offenses: violating 18 United States Code, Section 241 (conspiracy to interfere with a citizen's exercise and enjoyment of rights secured by the federal Constitution), by conspiring to release their victims from jail and then to intercept them and kill them, and violating Section 242 (willfully deprive a person under color of law of such rights by performing the acts contemplated in the conspiracy).

At trial, the district court held the indictment charging conspiracy was invalid as to all defendants on the ground that Section 241 did not include rights protected by the Fourteenth Amendment and that the second indictment was valid only as to the police officers among the defendants, dismissing it as to the nonofficial defendants. On appeal to the United States Supreme Court, the action of the district court was reversed; it was unanimously held that Section 241 covered assaults on rights guaranteed by the entire Constitution, including rights under the due process clause, and that under Section 242 private individuals were criminally liable if they were willfull participants in joint activity with the state or its agents.

PROTEST VIOLENCE

The black protest movement which had been concerned primarily with attempts to gain civil rights for blacks under constitutional guarantees was pressured by ghettoized blacks to shift to direct action likely to solve their economic and social problems. Leadership shifted from the old nonviolent men to those who were young and violence-oriented, and from groups such as the Student Nonviolent Coordinating Committee to the Black Panthers. Appeals to the white community and acquiescence to a white-dominated police force changed to demands based on the power of the black ghetto and defiance of police, and acceptance of police as protectors-with-guns was replaced by an arming of ghetto residents and planning defense strategy against official violence by police.

This switch to direct action and self-defense created an upheaval similar to the conflicts between management and labor in the first quarter of this century which led to the formation of America's trade unions and raised the socioeconomic levels of workingmen. It is also similar to the abolitionist movement of the nineteenth century which led to freedom for slaves. It is not only, however, a demand for freedom from slavery, but also a demand for equality of opportunity.[4]

Many black ghetto youths are now active in the Black Panthers and its radicalization of ghetto politics. Black Panthers want black liberation and a black renaissance, and their aim is to decolonize black ghettos. Decolonization, by nature, involves a violent meeting of two forces. The first encounter of white and black forces was slavery, and this exploitation of blacks was supported by force of arms. Decolonization is inherently a violence phenomenon.[5]

Young black people feel the political system has cheated them, and that it is only sustained in its present form by police-state tactics. For them, violence is a necessary by-product of the struggle for equality. They point out that violence has settled all historical issues for centuries.

It is an old myth that protest violence is spontaneous. It may not happen as planned, but it arises from a conviction among protestors that peaceful methods of adjustment are unlikely to succeed in obtaining their rights. Responsible officials should recognize protest violence as the sign of a desperate need for sweeping changes. Official violence in response to protest violence is likely to lead to greater violence as it does nothing to change the causative factors.

ALIENATION OF THE BLACK GHETTO

The black ghetto is not an adaptive device to ease its residents into the success routes and rewards of American life. It is a social mechanism which locks the black population into a subordinate status. Its liabilities include poor education, poor health, poor housing, and poverty.

Blacks in America have observed the criteria for white success. They feel their own aspirations are legitimate, and that it is grossly unfair to deprive them of equality and upward mobility. Many blacks have now

[4]Lee Rainwater and William L. Yancey, *The Moynihan Report and the Politics of Controversy* (Cambridge, Mass.: M.I.T. Press, 1967), pp. 47–50.

[5]Frantz Fanon, *Wretched of the Earth*, trans. by C. Farrington (New York: Grove Press, 1965), pp. 29–30.

acquired the education that is normally the key to occupational mobility and economic gain, but they have not achieved advancement or the related economic rewards. As a result, blacks feel unjustly deprived and protest or revolt to remedy the situation.

An overwhelming proportion of black ghetto residents suspects that the white-controlled complex of police, prosecutors, and courts does not deal justly with ghetto people. This general distrust focuses on police practices because of the visibility of police and their on-the-street confrontations with ghetto residents. This pervasive hostility to the legal system generally, and to the police particularly, contributes to ghetto violence. Most major incidents of ghetto violence have been responses to police action.[6]

The nature of ghetto violence from brick, stone, and bottle throwing to sniping and ambushing reflects the intense resentment of police by ghetto residents. Since much ghetto violence is expressive rather than instrumental, police casualties are not a true measure of the depth of the ghetto's alienation to the police.

Although this frame of reference may be caused by confinement to the ghetto and the general pattern of unemployment or low-wage employment, the overt causes are believed to be:

1. Blacks are the subject of police misconduct, harrassment, malpractice, and brutality.
2. Blacks believe the police are corrupt and enforce the law more vigorously in the ghetto than they do elsewhere.
3. Blacks are fatalistic about police behavior; they are convinced that blacks have no means to protest police misbehavior or inadequate law enforcement.[7]

Ghetto blacks do not view themselves as scapegoats or the white community as consciously racist; they see the police as an armed force representing the white community and using a legal system reeking with inequality and injustice to contain the blacks in the ghetto geographically, socially, and psychologically, as a subordinate, segregated people.

[6]Harlan Hahn and Joe R. Feagin, "Riot-Precipitating Police Practices: Attitudes in Urban Ghettos," *Phylon*, Summer 1970, pp. 183–93.

[7]Robert M. Fogelson, "From Resentment to Confrontation: The Police, the Negroes, and the Outbreak of the Nineteen-Sixties Riots," *Political Science Quarterly*, Vol. 82, No. 2, June 1968, pp. 217–47, p. 220.

CONFRONTATIONS: JACKSON, AUGUSTA, AND ORANGEBURG

Located in a black ghetto of Jackson, Mississippi, Jackson State College is primarily a school for black students. Most of the 4,000 students are residents of rural areas in Mississippi. Lynch Street, a major thoroughfare, cuts through the campus. Adjacent to the campus on Lynch Street is an area known as "the corner" frequented by local noncollege youths. White citizens of Jackson cross the campus on Lynch Street when traveling from downtown Jackson to white residential areas. Rock throwing on and near Lynch Street occurred in 1965 after a hit-and-run motorist seriously injured a Jackson State student; in 1966 with no known trigger event; in 1967 after police pursuit and apprehension on campus of a student traffic violator; in 1968 on the news of the assassination of Dr. Martin Luther King; and in 1969 when rumors of police brutality to blacks were spread on campus. In 1967 and 1968 violence escalated from rock throwing to arson, looting, and reported sniper fire, and official violence involved the use of shotguns by police. One black youth was found dead of buckshot wounds in 1967, and two students were injured by pellets from birdshot ammunition.

The 1970 violence at Jackson State was triggered by student reaction to official violence at Kent State University in Ohio on May 7, in which National Guardsmen shot and killed four white students. The violence began early in the evening of Wednesday, May 13, 1970. About 9:00 P.M. police received reports of rock throwing at motorists on Lynch Street. A responding Jackson City police car was struck by a missile and officers reported a crowd of 160–200 students. Roadblocks were established by police to seal the campus area and traffic was diverted.

At 11:00 P.M. the crowd had been supplemented by black, nonstudent youths from "the corner" area of the adjacent ghetto and police estimated the size of the crowd as about 700 men and women. The Mayor asked for mobilization of the National Guard and assistance from the state police (Mississippi Highway Patrol).

There was a march by a crowd of blacks on the ROTC building at about 11:15 P.M., but some students and faculty quieted and dispersed the crowd. Jackson City Police in force, with an armored vehicle purchased by a former mayor for riot control, moved to the campus. They were met with obscenities, and rocks were thrown at them. About midnight, local police were reinforced by state police units. By 1:00 A.M. the campus was quiet.

The campus remained quiet the next day, police opened Lynch Street to vehicle traffic, and several hundred National Guardsmen were billeted in a local armory about twenty minutes from the campus by car.

At about 9:30 P.M. events began to duplicate those of the previous evening: rocks were thrown, Lynch Street was closed, and the campus was sealed off by police. Tension in the crowd rose as rumors spread of official violence against blacks, and National Guardsmen were ordered to positions at the perimeter of the campus. The disorder escalated to bonfires and vehicle arson.

The city and state police formed a force of about sixty men, moved onto the campus, and formed a skirmish line in front of Stewart Hall, a dormitory. They faced jeers, insults, obscenities, and rocks and other missiles. The crowd refused police attempts at dispersal, and students obstructed firemen attempting to extinguish a vehicle fire and a large bonfire.

The police moved to disperse the students, now numbering about 300 to 400, and moved to Alexander Hall, another dormitory, where the street crowd was supplemented by students in open windows and doors. The police were met by more missiles as they closed the distance between themselves and the students. At short range the rocks and bottles thrown by students from windows of Alexander Hall and from the ground in front of the dormitory hit their targets, the police and police vehicles. Police fired shots from shotguns and other firearms.

In all more than 150 shots were fired. A student tape-recorded the firing noise and reported the barrage spanned twenty-eight seconds. The walls and windows of Alexander Hall were marked or pierced by hundreds of buckshot or bullets. (In shotgunning with buckshot, every shot fired dispatches nine to ten pea-sized projectiles toward the target.) Some of the firing was directed at students outside of Alexander Hall, but many shots were fired through doors and windows at students inside the dormitories. Two black students were killed and twelve other black students were wounded in this gunfire.

While officers later testified to shots fired by students, no physical evidence was found to support such testimony, and only one officer was wounded by gunfire (apparently by an almost-spent, flattened buckshot fired from a police shotgun which ricocheted). In any event, a 28-second barrage aimed at students in the windows and doors of Alexander Hall is not a legitimate response to sniper fire, nor was firing into the crowd of students outside of Alexander Hall a warranted response.

In the weeks that followed it was disclosed:

1. State police picked up empty shotgun shells at the shooting scene immediately after the barrage of gunfire. (The explanation was economy and training: on-the-range procedure at the state police academy required officers to pick up fired shells immediately and turn them in to the range officer for future reloading to lower the cost of ammunition for range practice.)

2. No police superior gave the order to open fire. (The claim was that confrontation at close range with blacks yelling obscenities was a new and infuriating experience for police and that the response to sniper fire was spontaneous.)

3. The governor of Mississippi, John Bell Williams, concluded that the police had resorted to firearms in self-preservation (and he expressed the assumption that the police did not instigate the problem or encourage it and that the blame must rest with the protestors).

4. Jackson police, through months of investigation by city officials, the FBI, a lawyer's committee, and a federal commission, claimed they had not fired at all. Later, in the friendly setting of a local grand jury inquiry, the deceit was disclosed and city police admitted firing their weapons.

5. The Hinds County Grand Jury accepted jurisdiction as Jackson is within county limits and reported that under the existing riot situation officers of both the Jackson police and highway patrol were justified in discharging their weapons and had used only that force necessary to protect themselves and to restore law and order on the campus of Jackson State College.

6. Black students at Jackson State perceive that years of protest have not led whites to respect the full human dignity of blacks and that the local effect of protest is only suicidal.[8]

The news reports of the two major confrontations at Augusta, Georgia, and Orangeburg, South Carolina, reveal a pattern of confrontation similar to the events at Jackson State: police response with violence and failure to place responsibility for wrongful deaths.

An unruly black crowd, angry because of the beating death on May 9, 1970, of a black youth in police custody, rioted in Augusta, Georgia, on May 12, 1970. There were fires, looting, and reported sniper fire. Six black men were shot and killed in a confrontation between police, rioters, and onlookers. Later, police admitted their shooting was responsible for five of the deaths (the other, by gunfire of "unknown" origin). None of the six killed were carrying firearms; three were reported to be bystanders; all, according to a state crime laboratory report on the autopsies, were shot in the back.

In September, a federal grand jury voted to indict two of the Augusta police involved in shooting one of the six victims. The charge was based on the federal law making it a misdemeanor to deprive a citizen of his "civil rights" and prohibiting police or any other person from inflicting "summary punishment without cause." Augusta Police Chief James G.

[8]President's Commission on Campus Unrest, *Campus Unrest* (Washington, D.C.: U.S. Government Printing Office, 1970), pp. 411–65.

Beck said he would not suspend the indicted officers but would keep them on duty because of the presumption of innocence until proven guilty. Governor Lester G. Maddox said, "at least the policemen restored law and order in Augusta."

On May 27, 1969, a federal court jury in Florence, South Carolina, acquitted nine state policemen charged with the death of three black students at South Carolina State College on February 8, 1968. The defendants were on trial for a misdemeanor under an 1870 federal law making it a crime to deprive a person of his constitutional rights—in this case, the right to live.

Government witnesses testified to the following major items of evidence:

1. Police were not provoked.
2. No warning was issued before police fired into a group of black students.
3. Several wounds were found in the backs and sides of the slain students.
4. Twenty-eight black students were also wounded by the police fire.

The defense claimed:

1. A highly dangerous and explosive situation existed on campus.
2. Defendants "did what they had to do" to combat an "armed mob" of rioters.
3. There was small-arms fire heard just before police opened fire (according to police and FBI-agent witnesses).

RIOTS

Riotous occasions may be described as minor civil disorders or major riots. A minor riot is characterized by: (1) a few fires (arson) and broken windows; (2) no more than twenty-four hours of rioting; (3) a small number of participants; (4) use of local or "mutual" police aid (from nearby localities). A major riot has the following characteristics: (1) many fires (arson); (2) extensive looting; (3) reports of sniping; (4) more than twenty-four hours of rioting; (5) crowds of onlookers; (6) use of state police, national guard, or federal military units.[9]

The pre-1940 riots in black ghettos were between local whites and black ghetto residents and were generally caused by socioeconomic friction between the two races. Police were usually reluctant peace-

[9] *Report of the National Advisory Commission on Civil Disorders* (Washington, D.C.: Government Printing Office, 1968), p. 65.

keepers who drove whites out of the black ghetto areas where the rioting occurred.

The East St. Louis riot of 1917 is characteristic of such earlier disturbances. Angered by the employment of black immigrants as strikebreakers, white mobs attacked blacks in downtown East St. Louis in early July. The rioters dragged their victims out of streetcars and then stoned, clubbed, kicked, and finally shot or lynched them. They also burned houses, and, with a deliberateness which shocked reporters, shot the black residents as they fled from the flames. The blacks, disarmed by the police and militia after an earlier riot and defenseless in their wooden shanties, could offer little resistance. By the time the East St. Louis massacre was over, the rioters had murdered at least thirty-nine blacks and wounded hundreds more. The government authorities, and especially the local police of East St. Louis, did not attempt to restore law and order with the firmness and impartiality exhibited by police in the riots of the 1960s.

In the Washington, D.C., riot of 1919, law enforcement in the capital broke down because the police were outnumbered (which is typical in American riots), and because the policemen appeared to sympathize with white rioters. Several hundred white sailors and some white civilians set out to avenge an alleged insult to a white sailor's wife. They prowled the Southwest Washington ghetto and attacked Negroes. Soon the white sailors were joined by white soldiers, and the assaults on blacks continued. The police, with a handful of military police reinforcements, provided scant protection for the terrified blacks.

The New York riots of 1935 and 1943, as well as the riots of the 1960s, were no longer whites against blacks, but blacks against police—a new direction for riots. Both riots were in Harlem, the site of New York's first black ghetto which dates from about 1910.

The 1935 riot began in a Harlem department store when a black youth was caught shoplifting and was forcibly subdued by employees. He was then taken to a back room and set free by the police. The black shoppers, however, believed that the police were beating the boy, and their fears were confirmed by the arrival of an ambulance called for an employee bitten in the scuffle. A crowd gathered quickly, and when someone parked a hearse nearby, the black shoppers concluded that the police had killed the youth. The police could not persuade them otherwise, and the rumor spread swiftly through the ghetto. Angry crowds looted and burned buildings and attacked police.

The 1943 riot erupted in a similar fashion in a Harlem hotel when a white patrolman attempted to arrest a black woman. A black soldier intervened, assaulting the officer with the officer's own nightstick, and in the struggle the patrolman shot his assailant in the shoulder. An ambulance removed the wounded soldier to a nearby hospital. The wound was not serious, but the rumor spread throughout Harlem that a white policeman had killed a black soldier. Again, fires, looting, and attacks on police resulted.

Possibly the common cause presented to both whites and blacks by World War II and the full employment of both races account for the quiet period between the 1940s and 1960s.

The 1965 Watts riot in Los Angeles was the first major civil disorder in which the cause of the riot was clearly the actions of an alienated black population. It was the reaction of ghetto residents who would no longer tolerate ghetto stores whose owners "bought cheap and sold dear," schools in which teachers helped black children fail, and grossly understaffed welfare units replete with red tape. They were frustrated, too, by a police department that harrassed instead of protected, and who tagged most of the black males with criminal records, and by a political leadership in Los Angeles that ignored blacks or responded inadequately to black needs.

Riots from 1966 to 1968 revealed clearly the same pattern of black ghetto residents plundering, torching, and battling police in a massive acting out against the liabilities of the ghetto. The typical post-1960 riot has the following major aspects: (1) accumulated grievances in the black ghetto; (2) trigger incidents; (3) private violence of rioters; (4) official violence of police and other repressive units; (5) police occupation of riot area.

The focus of riots since 1960 is generally directed toward police, looting, and destroying buildings. Rioters do not generally direct violence toward merchants in the area, but they may molest white motorists; they do not usually attempt any major acts of violence against persons outside the riot area.

THE 1967 DETROIT RIOT

Color-conscious official violence was evident in the 1967 Detroit riot. For over a year, the black ghetto residents in Detroit exhibited their unhappiness, but the local and state government responded only with armed police. Little was done to improve the conditions in Detroit's ghetto or the opportunity for social, economic, and political equality for its residents. Incidents leading to this riot were:

August 1966: A crowd formed during a routine arrest of several black youths in the Kercheval section of the city. Tensions were high for several hours, but no serious violence occurred.

June 1967: A black prostitute was shot to death on her front steps.

Rumors in the ghetto attributed the killing to a vice-squad officer. A police investigation later unearthed leads to a disgruntled pimp. No arrests were made.

June 26, 1967: A young black man on a picnic was shot to death while reportedly trying to protect his pregnant wife from assault by seven white youths. The wife witnessed the slaying and miscarried shortly thereafter. Of the white youths, only one was charged. The others were released.

July 23, 1967: Police raided a "blind pig," a type of night club in the ghetto which serves drinks after hours. Eighty persons were in the club attending a party for several servicemen, two of whom had recently returned from Vietnam. It was about 3 A.M., and a crowd of about 200 persons gathered as the police escorted the patrons into the police wagons. As the last police cars drove away from the "blind pig," the crowd began to throw rocks. By 8:00 A.M., looting had become widespread. Violence continued to increase throughout the day, and by 11:30 P.M. the crowd had reached 300 to 500 people. Shortly after midnight, window breaking and looting began.

The next day, Detroit counted 300 fires set on Sunday and an untold amount of looting. Entire blocks had been burned out. The city had now committed 600 policemen, supplemented by 350 state police and 900 National Guardsmen. Detroit's mayor and the governor of Michigan joined in a plea to the federal government for 5,000 federal soldiers. By nighttime, over thirty fires were burning out of control, looting was widespread, sniper fire was reported by police and firemen. There were several fatalities, including one National Guardsman.

On Tuesday, July 25, federal troops appeared on Detroit's streets. There was more burning, looting, and reported sniper fire. Hundreds of persons had now been arrested and were being held in improvised places of detention. Wednesday was one of the worst days. A white woman and a black child were killed, apparently by guardsmen allegedly responding to sniper fire. A fifty-calibre machine gun was fired by guardsmen into the building in which the child was fatally shot.

The homicides at the Algier's Motel also happened on the fourth day. Police arrived at the motel, reportedly in response to a radio alarm of sniper fire. They were familiar with the problems of the motel. Three young blacks were shot, and five blacks and two white girls were beaten. Later investigation disclosed that several of the responding police had taken the law into their own hands and used their shotguns as murder weapons. Eventually, the evidence centered on one police officer and directly linked him to two of the murders. There was compelling evidence that the three victims had been unarmed and unresisting at the time they were fatally shot.

On the fifth day, the rioting diminished, police and troops occupied the burned and looted sections of the ghetto, and a tally of the deaths, injuries, and property damage was made. The final figures were: 43 dead, 700 injured, $50 million property damage.

THE 1967 NEWARK RIOT

In the Newark, New Jersey, riot, only a few people were arrested as snipers, and no one was killed in possession of firearms or found dead under circumstances indicating that the deceased had been sniping. Twenty-four blacks and two whites died in the disturbance.

The riot began on July 12, 1967, and lasted five days. The trigger event was a normally unnoticed traffic dispute between the two occupants of a police car and a taxicab driver. The cabbie was arrested, and necessary force was used to subdue the arrestee and take him to the Fourth Precinct for booking and detention. Cabdriver friends of the arrested cabbie used their two-way radio network to complain. A crowd formed in front of the police station (in the center of the ghetto area), angry at first, then actively hostile toward police when news seeped out that the cabbie-prisoner had been severely beaten and taken to a hospital. Bricks, bottles, and stones began to fly at the police station windows. Police appeared in riot gear and cleared the street. A short time later, several fire bombs were hurled at the police station, scorching the walls, and the riot was on. Looting began and fires were set.

One report on official violence described how three carloads of Newark police stopped their cars in front of a six-story apartment house and confronted a crowd of black residents. When police opened fire with revolvers and shotguns, the crowd thought they were shooting blanks, but they then heard the impact of the bullets and buckshot on the apartment house's brick walls and the whine of some ricocheting projectiles.

Initial police reports said several looters ran in front of the crowd and police fired at the looters on the ground. In local riot commission hearings, police later claimed they were being shot at by snipers from the apartment house windows. According to the later report, police firing spanned no less than ten minutes. Several blacks in the crowd at ground level were wounded and one black was killed. The dead man had been struck by five double-O buckshot, four in the chest and one in the stomach. The prosecutor's investigation failed to identify the police involved.[10]

At one time on the third day of rioting, shooting had become so widespread among police and guardsmen that the police radio network broadcast the warning: "Hold your fire, you are shooting at your own men." Guardsmen who had been shooting at "snipers" on a roof were ordered to hold their fire because the snipers were actually policemen searching for snipers.

According to the Essex County prosecutor who investigated the riot's twenty-three criminal homicides, the problem of assigning blame for the deaths was complicated because 1,400 Newark police, 375 state police, and 3,000 New Jersey National Guardsmen were all active during the riot. In twenty-one or twenty-two homicides, Newark police, state police, or guardsmen had been pinpointed as the men firing guns, but many of them did not identify themselves as shooters. Ballistic tests of buckshot are usually futile in tracing the shotgun because the gun is unrifled (smooth bore) and does not leave rifling marks on buckshot as do rifles and revolvers. In any event, no cases against snipers developed, and no murder charges were brought against police or guardsmen.

The prosecutor presented his facts to the grand jury, and in a presentment dated nine months after the rioting, the conclusion of the twenty-three grand jurors, who had been given mute evidence of gunnery in autopsy reports but little evidence of whose hands held the guns, was, "In the final analysis, the responsibility for the loss of life and property that is the inevitable product of rioting and mass lawlessness cannot be placed on those whose duty it is to enforce law and protect the freedom of our society."[11]

A blue-ribbon commission to investigate charges of police brutality and to determine the causes of the rioting was appointed by New Jersey's Governor Richard A. Hughes. Seven hundred witnesses and five months later, the commission, now known as the Hughes Commission, published a suprisingly honest report. The riot was blamed on the social sickness that is the black ghetto, and the commission called for an investigation of the Newark Police Department, stating that some of the shooting reported as sniping was actually fired by police and guardsmen. The Hughes Commission had the following comment on the shooting and expenditures of ammunition during the riot:

[10]Ron Porambo, *No Cause for Indictment: An Autopsy of Newark* (New York: Holt, Rinehart & Winston, 1971), pp. 139–46.

[11]Porambo, *No Cause for Indictment,* pp. 217–18.

Although the State Police and the National Guard supplied an accounting for ammunition expended during the Newark disorders, the Newark Police Department has not been able to provide equivalent data. Director Spina [police] described the problem:

"Ordinarily it is very strict control, but during this disturbance it was absolutely impossible to keep tabulations of who you gave it to and in what quantities. We don't know to this day whether it was expended or whether it was in somebody's house, like shotgun shells, for example."

Police Inspector Henry [Newark Police Department] said that all ammunition had not yet been returned. He testified:

"The men are afraid that in the event we have another disturbance ammunition may not be available, or it may not be available in the quantity that is necessary, so they are holding on to what they have. They have got that put away. This I know for a fact."

Because of this and because of the use by Newark policemen of personal weapons that fired "whatever ammunition fitted those weapons" and because of the absence of an accounting system, the amount of ammunition expended by the police cannot be determined.

Upon request, State Police and National Guard authorities supplied ammunition reports to the Commission. Major Olaff [State police], in a report dated Dec. 29, provided an account based on a canvass of troop commanders. The report notes that no accurate figure of the number and type of ammunition expended can be determined because the urgency of the situation, limited time and insufficient manpower prevented keeping detailed records of how much ammunition was issued and expended. Furthermore, the situation in the field often required the free interchange of ammunition among the State Police, the Newark police and National Guardsmen. The report also states that the general sources for obtaining ammunition were the State Police and National Guard supplies. The approximation of ammunition expended by State Police personnel and set forth in the report was 350 rounds of 38-caliber; 1,168 of 45-caliber; 198 rounds of 00 buckshot; 1,187 rounds of 30-caliber, and 2 rounds of No. 9 birdshot.

On behalf of the National Guard, General Cantwell reported that a total of 10,414 rounds was the best estimate of ammunition expended: 10,198 rounds of 30-caliber rifle; 200 rounds of 30-caliber carbine; and 16 rounds of 45-caliber pistol.[12]

Table 4–1 provides an overall view of the circumstances of the deaths during the Newark riot of 1967.

[12]Governor's Select Commission on Civil Disorder [Hughes Commission], State of New Jersey, *Report for Action* (Trenton, N.J.: Governor's Office, 1968), p. 135.

Table 4–1. Homicides—Newark Riot

Date	Autopsy Report	Ballistic Report	Name	Age	Race	Location
7/15/67 11:45 A.M.	Homicide by shooting. Gunshot wound, right hip.	Insufficient characteristics for identification (1–.38 cal. bullet).	Rose Abraham	45	N	Brought to hospital by husband
7/14/67 4:30 A.M.	Homicide by shooting. Bullet wound right front chest. Indicates passed through.	Passed through.	Tedock Bell	28	N	Brought to hospital by friends
7/14/67 10:30 P.M.	Homicide by shooting. Bullet wound back of left chest.	Irregular lead fragment. No good for ID ("0" buckshot pellet).	Leroy Boyd	37	N	On sidewalk, Belmont & Avon
7/15/67 6:30 P.M.	Homicide by shooting. Bullet wound left abdomen.	NONE	Rebecca Brown	29	N	At home—in apt. window
7/14/67 5:30 A.M.	Auto accident. Fractured pelvis. Car she was in struck a fire engine.	....	Mary Helen Campbell	40	N	In a car at High & Spruce Sts.
7/14/67 5:30 P.M.	Homicide by shooting. Bullet wound left side of head.	Insufficient characteristics for identification (1–.38 cal. bullet).	Rufus Council	32	N	On sidewalk at 69 So. Orange Ave.
7/14/67	Homicide by shooting. Shotgun wound of chest and abdomen.	1–double "0" buckshot pellet no value.	Isaac Harrison	73	N	In the street at Springfield & Broome
7/14/67 7: A.M.	Homicide by shooting. Bullet wound back of head passed through.	.22-cal. bullet. 6 lands and 6 grooves, left twist.	Jessie Mae Jones	31	N	On her stoop, 255 Fairmount Ave.
7/15/67 2:55 P.M.	Homicide by shooting. Shotgun wound of back.	NONE	William Furr	24	N	On the sidewalk at 125 Avon Ave.
7/15/67 8: P.M.	Homicide by shooting. Bullet wound of left chest passed through.	Passed through.	Hattie Gainer	53	N	In her apt., 302 Hunterdon St.
7/18/67 1: A.M.	Homicide by shooting. Bullet wound of back of head passed through.	Passed through.	Raymond Gilmer	20	N	In the street at 744 Bergen St.
7/15/67 10:06 P.M.	Homicide by shooting. Shotgun wound, fractured skull front.	1 lead fragment no value for ID.	Rufus Hawk	24	N	At or near 949 Frelinghuysen Ave.
7/14/67 6:30 P.M.	Homicide by shooting. Bullet wound, right chest.	NONE	Oscar Hill	50	N	....

Date	Autopsy Report	Ballistic Report	Name	Age	Race	Location
7/14/67 7: P.M.	Homicide by shooting. 1 bullet wound, right arm. 1 bullet wound, back left chest.	NONE	Robert Martin	22	N	On the street at Broome & Mercer
7/14/67 11:55 P.M.	Homicide by shooting. Bullet wound in back, passed through.	Passed through.	Albert Mersier	20	N	On the sidewalk at 368 Mulberry St.
7/14/67 8:30 P.M.	Homicide by shooting. Bullet wound back of right ear, passed through.	Passed through.	Eddie Moss	10	N	Passenger in car at Hawthorne near Belmont
7/14/67 7: P.M.	Homicide by shooting. Bullet wound left chest, passed through, bullet wound left arm passed through.	Passed through.	Cornelius Murray	28	N	On the sidewalk, Jones near Springfield
7/17/67 12:50 P.M.	Homicide by shooting. Bullet wound of right abdomen, passed through.	Passed through	Michael Pugh	12	N	On the sidewalk in front of his home
7/16/67 5:15 P.M.	Homicide by shooting. Shotgun and bullet wounds of back.	5-.38 cal. bullets; 2 of the 5 bullets, insufficient characteristics for ID; 3 bullets with a rifling of 5 lands, five grooves, right twist; 17-00-12 gauge shotgun pellets leaving no rifling.	James Ruttledge	19	N	Inside of Jo-Rae Tavern, Bergen & Custer
7/15/67	Homicide by shooting. Shotgun wound left side of neck, passed through. Superficial wound on neck.	Passed through.	Eloise Spellman	41	N	Inside her apartment
7/14/67 4:10 A.M.	Homicide by shooting. Shotgun wounds back and left arm.	NONE	James Sanders	16	N	At or near Sampson's Liquor Store, Springfield & Jones
7/14/67 11:15 P.M.	Homicide by shooting. Shotgun wounds of back.	NONE	Richard Taliaferro	25	N	Leaving a store at So. 8th St. & 11th Ave.
7/14/67 7:30 P.M.	Homicide by shooting. Small caliber bullet wound, left chest.	.22 cal. lead (nose portion) bullet recovered.	Det. Fred Toto	33	W	Broome & Mercer Sts.
7/15/67 10:45 P.M.	Homicide by shooting. Bullet wound left flank, metalic bullet.	Core of .30–06 rifle bullet recovered. Not valid ID. Casing not recovered.	Capt. Michael Moran	41	W	At scene of a fire, Central & So. 7th St.

Source: Hughes Commission, *Report for Action*, pp. 138–39.

In a 1971 postmortem of the Newark riot, local reporter-writer Ron Porambo, linked police behavior during the riot with corruption in Newark's City Hall that surfaced in post-riot years revealing the improper activities of Newark's mayor, police commissioner, and other municipal officials. An FBI investigation proved that these officials worked with the local representatives of the *Cosa Nostra* to extort millions of dollars from building contractors and to accept similar sums to protect organized crime. In his book, *No Cause for Indictment: An Autopsy of Newark,* however, Porambo concludes that, although corrupt leadership was one factor in the excessive use of official force and in the no-prosecution whitewash, another important factor was the police and guardsmen who ignored standing orders regarding the legal use of firearms: "They executed petty thieves. They slaughtered women and children. They murdered innocent men. The jury's presentment amounted to a rubber stamp of approval for murder and manslaughter."[13]

THE 1968 CHICAGO RIOT

The 1968 Chicago riot had a death list of nine persons, six of whom died from bullet wounds of undetermined sources. The Chicago Riot Committee commented on the circumstances of several deaths:

> Four of the blacks who died during the evening of April 5, died under especially disturbing circumstances. All four were shot within a space of three and one-half hours during the evening. All four were shot within an area of two square blocks on Madison Street. . . . Two were shot from the street at 7:30 and 7:35 P.M., by rifle fire aimed into two stores crowded with looters at 4135 and 4113 West Madison Street. Two were shot in an alley parallel to and between West Madison and West Monroe Streets. None was resisting arrest according to the Committee's reasonably detailed and reliable information. Allegedly two police cars containing two to four white policemen in each car who were armed with rifles were in the two block area at this time and were seen shooting on the level into stores in these two blocks and shooting on the level in the alley in question.[14]

[13]Porambo, *No Cause for Indictment,* p. 247.

[14]Mayor's Riot Commission, *Chicago Riot Report* (Chicago: Office of the Mayor, 1967), pp. 36–37.

RAIDS AND SHOOT-OUTS

In the later 1960s, black power advocates began to influence their fellow blacks in ghettos. Malcolm X captured the imagination of many ghetto citizens, sacrificing his life for his beliefs. Later, the formation of the Black Panthers into a nationwide group with representatives in almost every ghetto provided a framework for protest. The leaders of the Black Panthers have been both literate and articulate; they have vocalized the unhappiness of ghetto blacks, and they have expressed a special antagonism for police and other law enforcement agents.

Law enforcement officials responded to the supposed threat of the Black Panthers by infiltrating the organization with spies and undercover police, by raiding Black Panther offices and residences, and by holding shoot-outs with the Panthers. The late FBI director J. Edgar Hoover described the Panthers as the greatest threat to America since Communism, and his agents passed "intelligence" on to local police about the Black Panthers and their operations.

This angry official response appears to have hardened black resistance and protest and to have accelerated the shift from spontaneous rioting to planned sniping and other terrorism. Rather than quelling the pressure for social change, official violence has helped to consolidate Black Panther membership. The aftermath of riots and violent acts may appear less expensive to the white community than the cost of desegregating ghettos and funding increased welfare, jobs, and housing for ghettos residents; the social costs of policemen and Panthers killed in raids and shoot-outs, however, are beyond measure.

SHOOT-OUT IN CLEVELAND: THE EVANS CASE

On July 23, 1968, Cleveland police placed two surveillance cars in the vicinity of the residence of Fred (Ahmed) Evans as the result of an FBI report to the police that Evans and his ghetto group, the Black Nationalists of New Libya, were assembling arms and ammunition in preparation for several simultaneous assassinations planned for July 24.

Evans and his group often displayed firearms, and Ohio law allowed possession of nonautomatic firearms. Early in 1967 police had arrested Evans for assault on a police officer and closed his place of business, The Afro Culture Shop and Bookstore, for "Sanitary Code violations."

The surveillance teams observed no unusual activity during the afternoon of July 23. Later investigation disclosed that Evans had asked two city councilmen who visited him about 6 P.M. why the cars full of white police were present and requested that they have the surveillance removed.[15] Shortly after the two councilmen left Evans, a police tow truck was sent to pick up an abandoned car in a street in Cleveland's black ghetto about two blocks from Evans's residence. As the two uniformed men alighted by the derelict car, assailants hidden nearby fired upon them. The tow truck driver was shot, and his assistant radioed for help. The injured man said, "The snipers set up the ambush and used the tow truck as a decoy to bring the police in. They had their crossfire all planned. We were sitting ducks."[16]

One of the police surveillance cars near the scene said it observed the tow truck operator running with his hands up and an armed black chasing him. Then the surveillance car was struck by gunfire. The two-man team in the surveillance car stopped and shot at the two snipers hiding behind the tow truck. Other police participated in this fight with three to four snipers, and the shooting soon spread to involve more blacks and police. At 8:30 P.M., the police broadcast a call for "all units." By 11:30 P.M., at least twenty-two people were killed or injured, with estimates of the police involved ranging from fifty to several hundred, and Evans surrendered to police in a house on the edge of the two-block shoot-out area.[17]

As the shooting diminished, however, the crowds of black onlookers resorted to rock throwing, looting, and arson which developed into five days of disorders. In a total of about eighty hours, three white policemen and eight black civilians were killed. Press reports described the shoot-out both as an ambush of police and an armed uprising by blacks.

Two months later a special report on the shoot-out by three reporters appeared in the *New York Times*.[18] It stated that the evidence indicates the Cleveland shoot-out was neither ambush nor uprising, but "spontaneous combustion," and that Evans said he was asleep at 6 P.M. when he was awakened by one of his group and told of the police surveillance. "So we armed ourselves" Evans reportedly said, "and what followed was chaos."

Evans was charged and convicted on seven counts of murder in an indictment alleging conspiracy. The prosecution presented the case as a conspiracy to kill police, the defense claimed it was a police attempt

[15]Louis H. Masotti and Jerome R. Corsi, *Shoot-out in Cleveland: Black Militants and the Police, A Report to the National Commission on the Causes and Prevention of Violence* (Washington, D.C.: U.S. Government Printing Office, 1969), pp. 44–47.

[16]Masotti and Corsi, *Shoot-out*, pp. 43–44.

[17]Masotti and Carsi, *Shoot-out*, pp. 47–50.

[18]Anthony Ripley, Thomas A. Johnson, and C. Gerald Fraser, "Cleveland Searches for Reasons for 4-Day Race Battle in July," *New York Times*, September 2, 1968.

to wipe out Evans and his following of black nationalists. Two key witnesses testified for the prosecution. One, a sergeant of the Cleveland Police Department's Subversive Squad testified the defendant Evans had told him that revolution was inevitable, and "sooner or later there's going to be open warfare between whites and blacks and the beasts [police] will be eliminated." The other witness, a seventeen-year-old black youth, testified to a meeting on the morning of July 23 at Evans's home at which a shoot-out with police was discussed, and Evans showed the group present "how to load and unload a rifle and what to do if it jammed." At the time of his testimony this second witness was under arrest pending trial for murder and arson arising from an event two months after the shoot-out. Later all charges against him were dropped.[19]

Although the argument that black militants planned an ambush and conspired to kill policemen was accepted by the jury, the defense theory has some supporting evidence. The Cleveland Police Department's Tactical Unit conducting the surveillance had initiated contact with the militants and did not warn the regular patrol force who responded of the armed confrontation; the tow truck happened to arrive on the scene at that time; and shooting of eight police within two minutes of police response to the tow truck operator's call indicates that responding police were unprepared to meet armed black militants. Two surveillance cars of the Tactical Unit were in the area of Evans's residence, manned by five men (Gerrity, Horgan, Gallagher, O'Malley, and Sweeney), yet the first two responding policemen shot were Officers McManahan and Czulkalski as they responded from regular patrol car 591. Then six more policemen were shot, none of whom were in either of the two surveillance cars.

THE CHICAGO BLACK PANTHER RAID: THE HAMPTON CASE

The Chicago Panther raid is likely to become a classic case in criminal justice literature. On December 4, 1969, at 4:04 A.M., a fourteen-man detail of Chicago police attached to the office of State Attorney (prosecutor) Edward V. Hanrahan raided an apartment in the West Side ghetto area occupied by Black Panthers. The police raiders had a warrant to search for weapons based on an FBI tip that the Black Panthers were stockpiling weapons.

---

[19]Roldo Bartimole, "Bad Day in Cleveland," *The Nation*, July 14, 1969, pp. 41–45, 61.

Police reported they were greeted by a hail of gunfire when they gave notice of their intent to serve a search warrant. Two local Panther leaders were killed: twenty-one-year-old Fred Hampton and twenty-two-year-old Mark Clark. Four other Panthers, including two women, were wounded. Police said six or seven Panthers were firing, and about 200 shots were exchanged in a 10-minute shoot-out. The leader of the police told newsmen after the raid, "I asked everyone to lay down their arms, and a voice from the back said, 'Shoot it out.' " Two policemen were injured slightly, one grazed by a bullet and another cut by flying glass. Seven surviving Panthers in the apartment were arrested and later indicted for attempted murder and unlawful use of weapons. Eighteen-year-old Brenda Harris was charged with firing a shotgun as police broke down the door and entered the apartment.

The Black Panthers claimed that Fred Hampton was shot while in bed, unarmed and that police had come in shooting and without warning. At a coroner's inquest into the deaths of Hampton and Clark, police witnesses discredited claims made by the Black Panthers and testified that the Black Panthers had opened fire first as the police forced their way into the apartment after being refused entry by the occupants. Later, at grand jury hearings, a criminalist of the Chicago Police Department Crime Laboratory reported two expended shotgun shells recovered in the apartment by police had been fired from a Black Panther weapon. Other police witnesses swore that at least one shot had been fired from this shotgun by Brenda Harris.

On May 8, 1970, over five months after the raid, State Attorney Hanrahan announced that all criminal charges against Miss Harris and the other Black Panthers arrested at the time of the Hampton-Clark raid were being dropped because of insufficient proof that any of the defendants had fired a weapon at police. Hanrahan's dismissal of charges was largely the result of a United States grand jury which had been convened to determine whether the police had violated the Panther's civil rights in the raid and shoot-out. The jury said that police had riddled the Panther apartment with eighty-two or more bullets and shotgun slugs. Only one shot had been fired from inside, and Miss Harris was exonerated of guilt in firing this single shot.

The police criminalist admitted to this jury that he knew his examination which linked the two expended shotgun shells with a Panther shotgun was inadequate, but his refusal to cooperate would have jeopardized his job, and he could not complain because it was the state attorney's office who had turned the evidence over to him. The autopsy surgeon who had testified at the coroner's inquest and before the county grand jury admitted he had been mistaken in his statements about the entrance and exit bullet wounds in his autopsy of Fred Hampton.

Most of the raiding policemen were transferred to other duties. Several high-ranking police and laboratory personnel were demoted and transferred, and three of Hanrahan's assistants were assigned to other duties—but no one was indicted by the federal grand jury.

Unhappy black nationalists called it a sophisticated whitewash; they refused to cooperate in the white-dominated federal investigation and had no faith in the jury composed of twenty-two whites and one black. Others described the grand jury action as a deal between the state and federal prosecutors. A police "shoot-in," doctored evidence, perjury, false official press releases (by police and prosecutor) describing the Black Panthers as the aggressors, and the death of two blacks —one apparently shot in bed—certainly seem to warrant more action than the departmental demotion or transfer of police and prosecutors involved.

Later in 1972, public reaction led to the appointment of a special prosecutor and an indictment for conspiracy to obstruct justice against Hanrahan and his raiders. The defendants were acquitted after a thirteen-week trial when the judge ruled that the evidence was not sufficient to establish any conspiracy.

Many police officers will view this lenient penalty for two deaths, now established as criminal homicides, as acquiescence to police persecution of the Black Panthers. The white community should be alerted that this tacit approval can easily lead to substituting police firepower for justice under law. Any sort of police conspiracy to deprive Black Panthers of their constitutional rights condoned by the white-dominated community marks the first awful step toward the loss of liberty for all citizens, white and nonwhite alike.[20]

THE CASTE SYSTEM

Although police raids and shoot-outs may succeed in seizing some firearms from ghetto blacks, such official violence can hardly be viewed as useful or practical. Unfortunately, the 1960 riots did not lead to the dismantling of the white-black caste system. Riot commissions were appointed to study the problem, but they did little to ameliorate the racist ideology which caused the riots. Some commissions assumed the task of exonerating police and guardsmen for their violence.[21]

---

[20]Don A. Schanche, *The Panther Paradox: A Liberal's Dilemma* (New York: David McKay, 1970), p. 226.

[21]Anthony M. Platt, ed. *The Politics of Riot Commissions: 1917–1970: A collection of Official Reports and Critical Essays* (New York: Macmillan, 1971), pp. 521–26.

For instance, the President's Commission on Campus Unrest, called the Scranton Commission after its chairman, drew the following conclusions from its study of the confrontation at Jackson State College:

1. There must not be a repetition of the "tragic incident" (three deaths).
2. Police should examine their policies on the use of buckshot rather than birdshot in police shotguns.
3. State police should reexamine the position that their rules on the use of firearms do not require correction.
4. Police and students should commit themselves to end the hostility that presently divides them before it happens again at Jackson State.

The Scranton Commission's report illustrates the politics of riot commissions and their intellectual and political failures. Initially a symbol of hope for political and social change, the commission ended by affirming established white institutions.

Social scientists have demonstrated that responsibility for the disadvantages blacks suffer in ghetto life rests squarely on the white community which derives economic and psychological benefits from the caste system. White cupidity leads to the poor quality of education and other services in the ghetto as well as low income for blacks and social stigmatization. In adapting to this setting, blacks perpetuate the harmful environment and also develop hostile feelings in response to discrimination, thus adding their own punishment to that inflicted by whites. The white caste system maintains a cadre of whites and middle-class blacks who function in refined or brutal ways to preserve the system (the KKK, the rural sheriff, municipal and state police, and the ghetto businessman). This coercion, both violent and subtle, is carefully concealed from the unprejudiced segment of the population whom it might offend.[22]

Because the state and local criminal justice systems have not effectively protected blacks from official violence, federal laws are used when state and local agents deny a citizen his constitutional rights. A recently rediscovered law, Title 42, U.S.C., Section 1983, a 1964 version of the Ku Klux Klan Act of 1871, is now being used as a legal remedy for damages resulting from color-conscious official violence. "Known as the Ku Klux Klan Act, the Anti-lynching Act, and the Third Civil Rights Act, this statute was designed to 'enforce the provisions of the Four-

---

[22]Lee Rainwater, *Behind Ghetto Walls: Black Families in a Federal Slum* (New York: Aldine-Atherton, 1970), pp. 3–4, 361–97. See also William H. Grier and Price M. Cobbs, *Black Rage* (New York: Basic Books, 1968).

teenth Amendment' and to halt the practices of organized bands of Caucasian southerners attempting to deprive the freedmen of their newly acquired rights."[23]

This statute was among three constitutional amendments and five civil rights acts conceived and passed by the Reconstruction Congress in the years immediately following the Civil War. Amended and re-amended, and now modified as section 1983 of Title 42 of the United States Code (U.S.C.), it reads:

> Every person who, under color of any statute, ordinance, regulation, custom, or usage, of any State or Territory, subjects, or causes to be subjected, any citizen of the United States or other person within the jurisdiction thereof to the deprivation of any rights, privileges, or immunities secured by the Constitution and laws, shall be liable to the party injured in an action at law, suit in equity, or other proper proceeding for redress.

Society has granted police license to violate the law in order to enforce it. They may kill when necessary and justified, invade privacy, and disregard other laws in the line of duty. The resultant sense of power may implant the idea that police are above the law. Official action in response to the private violence of civil protest should be restrained and police should avoid punitive actions; when protestors become alienated and fearful, disturbances escalate. In a democratic society police must not use coercion to sustain the social and economic dominance of one group at the expense of others or to inhibit constructive and corrective change.[24]

DISCUSSION QUESTIONS

1. Define official violence; private violence; color-conscious official violence.
2. Is there a subliminal fear among the white population (and its police, prosecutors, and judiciary) of a "slave rebellion"?
3. What common factors are found in the confrontations between police and blacks at Jackson, Augusta, and Orangeburg?

---

[23]"Socio-legal Aspects of Racially Motivated Police Misconduct," *Duke Law Journal*, Vol. 1971, pp. 751–83. See also Don Whitehead, *Attack on Terror: The FBI Against the Ku Klux Klan in Mississippi* (Funk & Wagnalls, 1970).

[24]Ralph W. Conant, *The Prospects for Revolution: A Study of Riots, Civil Disobedience and Insurrections in Contemporary America* (New York: Harper & Row, 1971), pp. 158–63.

4. What evidence has surfaced of police overreaction to sniper fire during the Detroit and Newark riots?

5. What is the caste system in America? Which individuals and groups perpetuate it and why?

CASE REFERENCE

United States v. *Price*, 383 U.S. 787 (1966).

5

Political Trials

A trial is termed "political" if the prosecutor hopes to gain political benefits from his successful prosecution, or if the prosecutor attempts to incriminate the defendant in order to discredit him politically. The actual innocence or guilt of the accused is of less importance in such a trial than the political ramifications of its outcome. Many argue that constitutional guarantees and a common respect for the law ensure that political issues are ignored in criminal proceedings because recognized trial standards include due process, fair trial, and equal treatment. The reality, however, is that the judicial process is often used to attain political goals and to influence the distribution of political power.[1]

[1]Otto Kirchheimer, *Political Justice: The Use of Legal Procedure for Political Ends* (Princeton, N.J.: Princeton University Press, 1961), pp. 46–48.

81

Political trials are usually directed against a member of a minority group who threatens to upset the status quo. The prosecutor operates in such cases under the assumption that the law itself, the enforcement of the law, or the police and courts do not fulfill their functions adequately. His actions are fostered by the same assumption that led to vigilantism and lynch law: when a community feels threatened or frustrated by some offense, it can grant virtual immunity for any retaliatory action. Thus prosecutors make deals with accomplice witnesses and use their testimony to provide details for a fictitious story proving the guilt of the defendant. They can also use mass conspiracy trials to legitimize otherwise inadmissible evidence and employ "hanging judges" who have lengthy records of being pro-prosecution to assure a verdict of guilty as charged.[2]

THE PROSECUTOR

Throughout the United States the county prosecutor, or district attorney[3] is the key law enforcement official. Police depend on him for assistance. The community views him as their representative in our adversary legal structure. Community confidence in a prosecutor's integrity and honesty allows him the decision to charge—whether or not to bring a case to trial. In addition, the prosecutor is officially known as the legal advisor to the grand jury and, unofficially, is the manipulator of this select group's indictments and the particular crime charged in the indictment.

It is a role with power which is sometimes misused. Years after a trial ending in a conviction, facts are developed which not only indicate that the defendant was innocent, but also show that the trial evidence was rigged, by suppression of evidence favorable to the defendant or by outright perjury.

COMMUNITY PREJUDICE

Community hostility toward the accused generally leads to political trials, since the prosecutor acts as community agent. The crime is likely to be a violent one, the suspect is usually poor, and he is generally one

[2]Roy Cohn, *A Fool for a Client: My Struggle Against the Power of a Public Prosecutor* (New York: Hawthorn Books, 1971), pp. 44–59, 164–72.

[3]The term originally indicated a prosecutor serving a district of more than one county; now it is synonymous with prosecutor.

of a minority. Life styles usually determine criminal behavior. The crimes of the rich are usually against property (income tax evasion; misappropriation of funds). They do not commit rape in freight cars or participate in bomb plots, and, if they did, there would be little hostility since members of the establishment would probably excuse the crime as the result of mental illness.

When a community is outraged, it is prejudicial, and hostility arises from a difference in class, religion, race, nationality, or in basic attitudes. This hostility affects not only the prosecutor but also the jurors. They feel a need to act in accordance with the disapproval of the masses.[4] In such a hostile environment, the community views the political trial as long overdue action against anarchists, radicals, and revolutionaries who threaten the climate of law and order in the community.

The treatment of Black Panther Bobby Seale in New Haven, Connecticut, on the eve of his murder trial reflected the hostility of the community and the impossibility of a fair trial; Kingman Brewster, President of Yale University, expressed his personal doubts about the situation: "I am appalled and ashamed that things should have come to such a pass that I am skeptical of the ability of black revolutionaries to achieve a fair trial anywhere in the United States."[5]

PERSECUTION VERSUS PROSECUTION

The prosecutor of Rio Arriba county in northern New Mexico was the object of an armed raid on the county courthouse. Reies Lopez Tijerina, a migrant laborer born in Texas, led the raid; his avowed purpose was to make a citizen's arrest of the prosecutor for unjustified prosecutions. Tijerina and his group represented the *Alianza*, a militant organization in the Southwest who for years had been demanding the return from the federal government and private owners of millions of acres of land. They believed the lands were legally theirs by right of the land grants given to their ancestors during the years of Spanish sovereignty and Mexican jurisdiction prior to the American takeover of this area under the 1848 Treaty of Guadalupe Hidalgo.

The civilian arrest of the prosecutor did not occur; instead there were two hours of shooting between the Mexican Americans and the

[4]Arthur Garfield Hays, *Trial By Prejudice* (New York: Da Capo Press, 1970; originally published in New York by Covici-Frede, 1933), p. 16.

[5]Haywood Burns, "Can a Black Man Get a Fair Trial in this Country?" *Law and Change in Modern America*, Joel B. and Mary H. Grossman, eds. (Pacific Palisades, Calif.: Goodyear, 1971), pp. 330–39

police. Tijerina and his followers fled to the mountains, seeking refuge with supporters of *Alianza*.

Government officials in New Mexico, previously embarrassed by Tijerina's talk of land speculators, and United States territorial officials, who seized the land in the 1880s when its potential for cattle grazing was first recognized, moved promptly, and the manhunt began. Tijerina and his followers were hunted down, arrested, and brought to trial. The courthouse raid was a general protest against the government refusal to adjust *Alianza* grievances, and a specific protest against the local prosecutor for harrassing the *Alianza* by various arrests and prosecutions.[6]

Another case, in 1942 during World War II, originated in a conflict between military service personnel and Mexican American youths in Los Angeles. The youths had adopted the zoot suit of Eastern teenagers: long tight-waisted coats, pleated pants, and lengthy chains dangling from their belts. The Mexican American zoot suiters were viewed as persons avoiding military service in time of war. The servicemen, many of whom were drafted into the military, began the hostilities; the youths responded, and the community sided with the military. The hostility of the community to zoot suiters, now a term applied to all Mexican Americans in the fifteen to twenty-four age group in Los Angeles, led to a mass murder conspiracy prosecution, later reversed on appellate review.

This political trial was an apparent reaction by the prosecutor to public clamor for a victim. Known as the "Sleepy Lagoon" case in the Los Angeles press, twenty-two zoot suiters, all Mexican American youths from poor families in the Los Angeles *barrio*, were charged with assault causing the death of a youth. At the mass trial of the twenty-two defendants, three of the youths were convicted of first-degree murder, nine found guilty of second-degree murder, five guilty of assault, and five were acquitted. The twelve defendants found guilty of murder, however, won reversals of their convictions on appeal.[7]

The four defendants in the Scottsboro Boys case in South Carolina were prosecuted because of their race and the community sentiment that they should be punished despite little compelling evidence of guilt. The case against the Scottsboro boys was the joint rape of a white girl. The crime occured on March 24, 1931. On the same day, police arrested nine black boys between thirteen and twenty years of age as "responsibles" for this assault and rape. Trials started on April 6, 1931, and were

[6]Peter Nabokov, *Tijerina and the Courthouse Raid* (Albuquerque, New Mexico: University of New Mexico Press, 1969), pp. 13–16.

[7]*People* v. *Zammora*, 152 P. 2d 180 (Calif.) (1942).

over within a week. Four of the older boys were found guilty and sentenced to death. On November 7, 1932, the U.S. Supreme Court reversed the trial court's conviction (and its affirmation by Alabama's highest court), saying it was their opinion that the defendants had not been given a fair opportunity to secure counsel of their own choosing and the counsel assigned by the court to the boys' defense did not contribute effective and substantial aid to the defense case.[8]

The indictment and trial of Bobby Seale on charges of conspiring with others in a kidnapping and murder in Connecticut were no doubt connected with the facts that he was black and an official of the Black Panthers. Connecticut's criminal procedure was criticized by the defense attorney, Charles Garry, in his examination of the local sheriff responsible for summoning the grand jury that returned the indictment of Seale and his conspirators. This damning expose took only a few minutes.

Mr. Garry was questioned by the presiding judge about the direction of his questioning of the sheriff. Garry explained he was attempting to show that the method of selecting grand jurors was haphazard and represented known cronies of the sheriff more than a cross section of the community. In response, the judge summed up the sheriff's answers to prior questions: "He talks to people who have decent reputations and they recommend people of decent reputations. Then he picks some of these people, and this is the way he does it."

Then Mr. Garry queried the sheriff as follows:

Q—You heard what the judge said?
A—Yes.
Q—Is that what you stated?
A—That is what I meant.
Q—You did not state that you yourself picked people who had decent reputations?
A—People who recommend them to me are people of good reputation.
Q—In other words, if a person has a decent reputation, and recommends someone, you assume that he has a decent reputation, that the person who has been recommended by that person or friend of yours has the decent reputation?
A—Yes.

After this showing of a selection of grand jurors by crony, the sheriff was questioned by Mr. Garry.

[8] *Powell* v. *Alabama,* 287 U.S. 45 (1932).

Q—Sir, is there any reason why you have not prepared a random list
so that the grand jury can be called from a cross section of the community
without any basis of knowing the individuals personally?

The prosecutor objected, the objection was sustained by the presiding
judge; the question was not answered.[9]

In New York, twenty-two Black Panthers were arrested in 1969 and
charged with conspiracy to bomb several major department stores, two
railroads, and four police stations. The bomb-plot case charged a plan
of indiscriminate terrorism by the Panther group against the community. Most of the defendants waited ten months and more in jail because
they could not raise the $100,000 set as bail. Eventually, thirteen defen-
dants were brought to trial.

Undercover policemen who had infiltrated the Black Panthers were
major witnesses. They stated that the defendants looked over numerous
locations to find the best places for fire bombs, dynamite, and other
explosives, and that D day was the coming Easter weekend. The trial
jury suspected the undercover agents of being more eager to obtain
convictions than to report their observations accurately. The policemen
inflated the wishful plotting of individuals trapped by their environment and subordinate status into a serious revolutionary threat which
did not exist. When these witnesses reported no clinching evidence of
a defendant placing dynamite anywhere or agreeing to take such action, the jury voted to acquit.[10] The prompt acquittal suggests that the
New York prosecutor waited months before going to trial because he
knew he had a poor case.

THE CONSPIRACY CASE

A conspiracy case is based on talk, agreements and acts which further
a plot. In such a case, the prosecutor has the advantage. Evidence which
would be inadmissible at most trials is allowed in a conspiracy trial, and,
although there may be formal judicial instruction of how the jury should
consider it, once the jury has heard such evidence, it will influence the
decision on guilt or innocence.

Evidence in a conspiracy case is usually developed through the testimony of accomplice witnesses (commonly noticed by judges as rather

[9]Sara Blackburn, *White Justice: Black Experience Today in America's Courtrooms*
(New York; Harper & Row, 1971), pp. 277–89.
[10]Edwin Kennebeck, "Not Guilty of What," *The Nation*, 4 October 1971, pp. 296–304.

disreputable persons), infiltrators, spies, or undercover agents. Since such roles usually reveal an interested rather than a disinterested witness, it is little wonder that transcripts of conspiracy trials reveal perjured evidence or testimony in which significant facts are suppressed or "colored" to match the story line of the prosecutor's theory of conspiracy.

The Connecticut Bobby Seale case involved a Black Panther who had been exposed as a police spy and killed. In attempting to put together a conspiracy case which would include Seale, a high official of the Black Panthers, the prosecution ruined a good murder case against one or more of the conspirators against whom the state had compelling evidence to indicate their presence at the murder scene at the time of the crime. The trial jury did not believe the testimony of accomplice witness.

In the New York Black Panther case, the conspiracy had never gone beyond feasibility planning. However, there was sufficient testimony by undercover police to establish various overt acts to further the conspiracy. Normally, such evidence would result in a guilty verdict, but the jury did not believe the undercover agents and apparently discounted the truthfulness of most of their testimony.

In mass trials, one or more participants in the alleged crime are used to develop evidence of a conspiracy. In the prosecution of twenty-two defendants in the case of *People* v. *Zammora*,[11] the prosecution developed the conspiracy theory because defendants returned to the place of the crime after a fist fight with the "Downey boys" in which the zoot-suited defendants had been beaten. The prosecution's theory was that the defendants had entered into an unlawful combination or conspiracy in order to commit murder in satisfaction of their lust for revenge.

The twenty-two defendants were jointly charged by an indictment returned by the Grand Jury of Los Angeles County with murder (count 1) and with assault with a deadly weapon with intent to commit murder (counts 2 and 3). After entry of not-guilty pleas by all defendants on all counts of the indictment, trial before a jury resulted in the acquittal of five defendants on all three counts. Of the remaining defendants, five were acquitted of murder, but convicted of minor offenses necessarily included in the remaining two counts. The other twelve defendants were convicted on all three counts; three were found guilty of murder in the first degree and nine of murder in the second degree. These

[11]152 P. 2d 180 (Calif) (1942).

twelve defendants appealed. The California Court of Appeals reversed the conviction of the twelve appellants, remanding the case for a new trial.

The appellate court opinion's comment on the conspiracy theory of the prosecution was:

> At all events, it can be said that the evidence does not reflect any unanimity of purpose. There is some testimony that one of the defendants, who had previously been at the party and had danced with one of the Delgadillo girls, stated that it was a "good party" and suggested that they go there. There is other evidence that, when defendants Leyvas and some of his co-defendants entered upon the Delgadillo premises, they demanded to know the whereabouts of the "men who had beaten them up." Some of the defendants had no knowledge of the party and no longer expected to find the "Downey Boys," but just followed the others. But it belies the record to assert that what happened subsequently at the Delgadillo party was the result of a collective intent upon the part of the defendants to commit murder, and that the conduct, behavior, and actions upon the part of the defendants at the party manifested a conspiracy to commit murder or assault with intent to commit murder.[12]

TESTIMONY OF ACCOMPLICE
WITNESSES AND INFILTRATORS

The credibility of a witness can be evaluated by determining whether he has any motive to lie and whether he is the kind of person who might lie. An accomplice is a person involved in crime. He has been arrested or fears arrest; he is aware of the possibility of conviction and the law's penalty. Perhaps the prosecutor will offer him the opportunity to become a witness for the state. In return, the prosecutor will lessen the charge, not prosecute at all, or intercede to reduce the sentence. Faced with years in prison, sometimes knowing of prison conditions from past experiences, and the alternative of freedom, the witness is easily tempted to join the prosecutor's side. Such motivation obviously puts the accomplice witness in the *interested* category, rather than the *disinterested* witness group. Legal history is replete with the perjury of interested witnesses.

Police have developed a variety of clandestine investigative techniques to uncover leads which will solve crimes and secure evidence of guilt. Informers are a prime source of leads and are protected by the *informer's privilege* that police need not divulge the source of their

---

[12] *People* v. *Zammora*, pp. 185, 198.

information at the trial of a person arrested and charged as a result of the informant's confidential tales to police unless such divulgence of identity is required to ensure a fair trial for the defendant.

Spies are nonpolicemen paid to gather the information and usually use their own identity in the infiltration. Police undercover agents use an assumed name and a fictitious story, or "cover." Infiltrators may be distinguished generally by:

1. Function assigned or performed
2. Criminal justice agency which employs them
3. Criminal activity being investigated
4. Accompanying electronic gadgetry carried.[13]

In the New York City Black Panther bomb plot trial, the spy who obtained initial data to secure judicial approval of electronic surveillances was a person with a long history of mental illness, an extensive arrest record, and numerous aliases. He was paid $100 a week. The unreliability of this infiltrator, described at the trial as a "confidential informant," was stressed when police witnesses admitted a great deal of false information was given police.

In other cases, police undercover agents have been cross-examined by defense counsel as to whether they were instigators as well as infiltrators and whether the purchase of dynamite and the provision of cars and other aids to the conspiracy by the police agent were not actions beyond the legal limits of entrapment. Sometimes employment in the role of undercover police agent will influence the conduct and credibility of the role player's later testimony. The major police undercover agent in the New York Black Panther trial had worked in this role from 1964 to 1970, infiltrating several dissident minority group organizations. The refusal of the jury to accept the testimony of this police agent was probably because of the lengthy period of his work assignment.

Secret agents threaten free speech and free political debate. It is certainly not a free society when members of political or quasi-political groups, who are not in any conspiracy or illegal activity, must be wary of speaking to a secret government agent disguised as a friend.

THE PRO-PROSECUTION JUDGE

There is little doubt that the prosecutor attempts to bring the case before a judge who will reflect the hostility of the community and who

---

[13]Joseph R. Lundy, "The Invisible Police," *The Nation*, 8 December 1969, pp. 629–32.

might become his active ally. The assigned judge in the New York City Black Panther bomb plot case was alleged by one of the defense counsel to have been handpicked by the local prosecutor. Another defense counsel revealed that this judge's claim in open court that he was assigned to the case by the state's appellate division was false. Despite defense pleas, the judge remained. Although he may not have been handpicked, from the first day of judicial supervision he did act a pro-prosecution judicial role: the defense counsel was blamed for trial delays and charged with various poor practices from incompetence to contempt of court.

In their appeal of the Sleepy Lagoon case, *People* v. *Zammora*, counsel for the twelve Mexican Americans convicted of first- and second-degree murder claimed that the trial judge made numerous prejudicial remarks during the trial.

The record discloses the following dialogue:

Mr. Van Tress (defense counsel): I object to counsel leading the witness.

The Court: I would suggest, Mr. Van Tress, you having made repeatedly the objection that a question is leading, will you please look up during the noon hour just what a leading question is.

Mr. Van Tress: I have not made repeated objections.

The Court: I am sorry.

Mr. Van Tress: I have kept quiet for three days; I haven't repeated objections.

The Court: Somebody is using ventriloquism: we have a Charlie McCarthy using Mr. Van Tress's voice.

Mr. Shibley (also a defense counsel): I am going to assign that remark of your Honor as error.

The Court: You can assign it as error. I am getting thoroughly tired of useless and unnecessary objections being made in these proceedings. There is some reason back of the making of these repeated objections.

On another occasion when the same defense counsel made a statement to the court the following occurred.

The Court: Mr. Van Tress, I am afraid you have been asleep. The discussion now is as to whether the witness testified he did not feel it.

Mr. Van Tress: I resent the court's remarks I must have been asleep, because I have not been asleep.

The Court: You evidently did not hear what has been going on in the last five minutes.

Mr. Shibley: I think that should be assigned as misconduct.

The Court: Go ahead and make your assignment of misconduct. It is about time for you to make another one, anyway.

Mr. Shibley: And I ask the jury be instructed to disregard that. I also assign this last remark of the court as misconduct and ask the court to admonish the jury to disregard that too.

The Court: I am not going to give that instruction on either assignment, and I want the record to show that every time I caution counsel, or that he is told to pay attention to anything, or I indicate as to something which counsel himself should observe, Mr. Shibley immediately comes forward with an assignment of misconduct. You may proceed.

Viewed from the jury box, there is little doubt that every remark made by the judge and his every act during the trial are subjected to comment by the jurors. Invariably they will arrive at a conclusion based on what the court thinks about the case.

THE ALLEN CHARGE

Judges in political trials are sometimes confronted with a jury which cannot reach a verdict and returns to the court for further instructions. The trial judge may reinstruct the jury with what is known as the *Allen charge*, judicial instruction advising jurors to defer to the views of the majority. The name is derived from the case of *Allen* v. *United States.*[14] It is also termed the "dynamite charge" and "shotgun instructions." Because the defendant must be released when the jury cannot reach a verdict, the Allen charge is more likely to be used by a judge intent on forcing the holdouts against conviction on a jury into agreement with the majority in favor of conviction.

The Court's opinion in *Allen* reveals the pro-prosecution judicial instructions were:

That in a large proportion of cases absolute certainty could not be expected; that although the verdict must be the verdict of each individual juror, and not a mere acquiescence in the conclusion of his fellows, yet they should examine the question submitted with candor and with a proper regard and deference to the opinions of each other; that it was their duty to decide the case if they could conscientiously do so; that they should listen, with a disposition to be convinced, to each other's arguments; that, if much the larger number were for conviction, a dissenting juror should consider whether his doubt was a reasonable one which made no impression upon the minds of so many men, equally honest, equally intelligent with himself. If, upon the other hand, the majority was

[14]164 U.S. 492 (1896).

for acquittal, the minority ought to ask themselves whether they might not reasonably doubt the correctness of a judgement which was not concurred in by the majority.[15]

Two factors imply that these instructions were used mainly to overcome jurors holding out for acquittal. First, the Allen case had a history of faulty judicial instructions. In two previous trials, Allen's conviction was reversed on the grounds of error in judicial instructions. His third conviction was appealed on the same grounds, and, despite the fact that the decision went against Allen, the case is identified with error in judicial instructions. Second, the content of such judicial instructions seriously threatens the doctrine that innocence is presumed and the defendant should be acquitted unless proven guilty beyond a reasonable doubt.

DISCUSSION QUESTIONS

1. What are the factors likely to create a political trial? What are the characteristics of these trials?
2. Which common factors are found in the "Sleepy Lagoon" trial in Los Angeles and the Black Panther trial in New York?
3. Why is the testimony of an accomplice witness suspect? an undercover police agent? a paid "spy"?
4. What are the problems in defending members of disadvantaged minorities who are innocent of the crime charged?
5. Describe the Allen or dynamite charge.

CASE REFERENCES

Allen v. *United States,* 164 U.S. 492 (1896).
People v. *Zammora,* 152 P. 2d 180 (Calif.) (1942).
Powell v. *Alabama,* 287 U.S. 45 (1932).

[15]*Allen* v. *United States,* 164 U.S. 492 (1896), p. 501.

6

Discrimination in Correctional Systems

Reformers of the correctional system in the 1940s and 1950s said that the system was inadequate and ineffective. They charged that the prisons were dehumanizing warehouses which confined men with no attempts at rehabilitating them. The emphasis has recently attempted to pinpoint the problem area of racial and ethnic discrimination in the administration of prisons and by probation and parole personnel.

During the 1960s correctional staffs and prison administrations were plagued by fear, anxiety, frustration, and overreaction in their attempts to deal justly with black and brown inmates. Confusion, discrimination, bias, and repression became common in prisons, and inmates retaliated with strikes, riots, killings, and sabotage.

There are many factors contributing to these problems. The character and attitudes of the prison population are changing at a rapid rate and are influenced by the rise of the black power movement, the Mexican American *La Causa* and *La Raza* ideology, and the attempts of minority groups to improve education and their political and social position. Each minority has become more aware of its human and civil rights, and is making articulate and vocal demands on the whole correctional system.

Correctional systems, from probation through prisons to parole, are responsible in this country for the constructive management and re-socialization of inmates representing every racial and ethnic group in the society. One factor not readily recognized is that inmates from these minority groups bring to prison myriad negative encounters with the criminal justice system. These experiences involve attitudes, feeling, prejudices, and cultural patterns identical to those found in society at large. It is therefore virtually impossible to consider the operations of a prison or probation or parole agency without being aware of the economic, social, and political climate in which the agency functions. Prisoners are responding to the same forces as free people; as blacks, Chicanos, Puerto Ricans, and other minorities are becoming more militant and less willing to accept discipline and repression, so, too, are prisoners.

For most whites, prison remains a strange and unfamiliar phenomenon since relatively few whites go to prison or jail. For black and brown people, however, the prison is a pervasive element of ghetto life. Some ghetto parents talk of the different prisons in which their children are confined in the same way middle-class whites talk of the colleges their children attend. Prison is central to the black and brown experience because it is the culmination of many other repressive and discriminatory forces in society.

The process begins with the white policeman on the beat shaking down and cursing at the black or brown youth, and it continues through segregated, spirit-blighting, nonbilingual schools, through the juvenile court, through meaningless and dead-end jobs, demeaning welfare policies, the adult court, and the probation officer. The administrators are usually white, and the subjects black or brown. For this reason, today's prisons are inevitably shaken as society tries to move, though convulsively and disappointingly, toward a degree of equality and justice.[1]

[1]Herman Schwartz, "Prisoner's Rights: Some Hopes and Realities," *A Program for Prison Reform: The Final Report,* Annual Chief Justice Earl Warren Conference (Cambridge, Mass. Roscoe Pound—American Trial Lawyers Foundation, 1973), pp. 47–62, p. 49.

PRISONS AND PRISON PERSONNEL

For economic and political reasons, prisons are often located far from urban areas in rural communities where the economy needs a boost. Correctional officers are chosen from the extremely conservative residents of these rural areas; they become guards for economic reasons, pensions, and often as a second job to a farm or other occupation. Many officers staffing custody units are also recruited from the ranks of retired military personnel. These people usually have no understanding or sympathy for the urban blacks and browns, their unfamiliar life styles, their demands, and their resentments.

Custodial personnel are seen by prisoners, and often see themselves, as policemen. Their uniforms, paramilitary organization, and billy clubs reinforce that perception. In their union utterances and elsewhere, the guards often express a kinship and solidarity with law enforcement officers, and police, in turn, have explicitly affirmed their solidarity with the guard personnel of many prisons.[2]

The high percentage of black and brown inmates must face a prison custody personnel, many of whom are racially biased and who have the power to make decisions concerning the inmates' daily mode of living, personal convictions and beliefs, and sometimes their lives. Racist guards and white inmates may join together in verbal or physical attacks on nonwhite inmates to injure them or to provoke them into action for which they can be disciplined. The paid employee and the prisoner align because of their whiteness and the depth of their racial prejudice.

In California, wardens and superintendents (always identified with custody) have placed severe restrictions on the Black Muslims because they proselytized their antiwhite views in the prison yard. The guards said this was an incitement to violence and a threat to prison discipline. Although the Muslims claim they are a religious organization, the wardens said they were a social and political group in reality.

A Black Caucus of the California Assembly visited Soledad prison because of a conflict between prison staff and black and brown inmates which resulted in the tragic deaths of three inmates. The following extracts from the published report of these black assemblymen and senators illustrate the possible dimensions of racial discrimination in any prison in the United States:

[2]Schwartz, "Prisoner's Rights," p. 50.

The Setting: "O" Wing of Soledad Prison is the maximum security section, reserved for the most difficult inmates. Prison authorities call it "The Adjustment Center." Cells are 6 feet by 10 feet, one inmate to a cell. Three sides of each cell are solid wall; the door is not only barred but also covered with heavy steel mesh. Food is pushed through a slot at meal times. Men on "O" wing must remain in their cells 23½ hours a day, with 30 minutes reserved for showering and exercise. Inmates are deprived of normal prison privileges such as television, work, study, recreation, etc. For several months before January of 1970, inmates of "O" wing had not been permitted to exercise in groups because of racial tension between blacks on the one hand and whites and Mexican Americans on the other. At the same time, a new exercise yard had been constructed for inmates of "O" Wing.

The Happening: On the day the new exercise yard was opened, January 13, 1970, a group of 13 inmates—each one thoroughly searched to be sure he possessed no weapons—was released into the yard. One guard, O. G. Miller, was stationed in a tower thirteen feet above the yard, armed with a loaded carbine. After a fist fight broke out, Miller fired four times, killing three black inmates and wounding one white prisoner. Prison authorities maintain a warning shot was fired; inmates who were in the yard maintain there was none.

The Investigation: The District Attorney of Monterey County (where the prison is located) pronounced the killings justifiable homicide, and the Monterey County Grand Jury, after hearings at Soledad, found the shootings to be justifiable homicide.

The Letters: After the investigation absolved O. G. Miller, several legislators received letters expressing concern that no biracial commission had investigated the matter. Several inmates who had been in the yard when the killings took place wrote to various attorneys in California describing what they had seen. These letters contradicted the statements of prison authorities and described steady harassment of black inmates by correctional officers as well as by white inmates. This harassment, they reported, takes the form of racial epithets and slurs, contamination of food, and provocation by both correctional officers and inmates, and peaked out in the exercise-yard slayings.

Letter 1

On the morning of January 13 of 1970 we were all skin searched before being singularly released to the O-wing yard, seven Blacks and eight Caucasian, Mexican, and Polynesian inmates, ALL anti-Black; approximately thirty-five prison guards were in the immediate area as onlookers and assisting in the yard release. They were armed with various types of tear gas, billie clubs and flashlights which was more than enough to handle the fifteen inmates on the yard which was the total number of all of us, Blacks and non-Blacks. They knew that a battle was inevitable considering all that has been done to us by these inmates, they [the officials] manipulated and perpetrated the entire situation and kept us segregated from them and selected the Blacks to be assassinated, then used a fist fight to cover it; there was no gang fight as was reported to the news media; only seven inmates actually engaged in physical combat to the best of my knowledge.

The fight started between A [black] and another inmate [anti-black] who had race-talked and threatened him personally on the night of January 12 of 1970. The first shot killed A, who was only a few feet from me and as I turned to go to him and see how bad he was hurt and to protect him from being assaulted while he was down by the inmate he was fighting, B and C [blacks] who was only a short distance from me yelled to me to watch out and I turned to face the attack directed at me by two Caucasian inmates who was running towards me. B started for A to presumably see how bad he was hurt and to protect him from being attacked while he was down but he was shot dead a few feet from A before he reached him and C was shot dead trying to come to my assistance.

There were NO warnings of any kind given before the shooting, there was NO ganging up on any inmate by Blacks. The guard in the tower leaned out of the window with his gun at the ready from the time the first Black inmate arrived on the yard up until everyone was removed from the yard. The presence of approximately thirty-five officials and their armament was sufficient to break up the fight without a single shot being fired.

Letter 2

I looked at the tower guard and he was aiming the gun toward me and I thought then that he meant to kill me too, so I moved from the wall as he fired and went over to stand over inmate C, all the time looking the guard in the gun tower in the face.

He aimed the gun at me again and I just froze and waited for him to fire, but he held his fire. After I saw he was not going to fire, I pointed to where inmate C lay, with two other Black inmates bending over him, and started to walk to him very slowly. The inmate I had played handball with suggested that I take inmate C to the hospital so I kneeled so inmate C could be placed on my shoulder, then started to walk toward the door through which we had entered the yard, and the tower guard pointed the gun at me and shook his head.

I stopped and begged him for approximately ten minutes to let me take C to the hospital but all he did was shake his head. Then I started forward with tears in my eyes, expecting to be shot down every second. The tower guard told me, "That's far enough." Then another guard gave me permission to bring C off the yard and I was ordered to lay him on the floor in the officers' area and go to my cell, which I refused to do until C was taken to the hospital.

Letter 3

Anyway, on the 19th, I left for Sacramento, it was a Friday and I didn't return until Tuesday the 23rd. I was put in the same cell. It was the same environment—the air stayed stuffed with "Nigger here," and "Nigger there." On the 28th of December, a list was passed out announcing the opening of the Max Row yard on the 29th. But it didn't open because there was still some work yet to be done. But I did notice that white inmates and officials were awfully cheerful for some reason or another and they continuously didn't forget to remind us of the yard opening soon. . . . *Another inmate* kept telling me that these officials were up to no good and the white inmates would pass my cell asking me, "Are you coming out when the yard opens?" Most of the time I would laugh at them and sometime I would just sigh and roll on my other side trying to sleep. *Letter 4*

Never more than six Blacks were allowed on max row which houses twenty-four inmates, thus the remaining eighteen cells were occupied by anti-Black Caucasian and Mexican inmates who race-talk us in shifts so that it's done twenty-four hours a day. On their exercise periods they spit, throw urine and feces in our cells while the officials stand by in indifference and approval. The prison officials here stopped serving the meals and deliberately selected the Caucasian and Mexican inmates to serve the meals and they immediately proceeded to poison our meals by filling food to be issued to us with cleanser powder, crushed up glass, spit, urine, and feces while the officials stood by and laughed.[3]

The circumstances described above should not be considered isolated events; they have occurred elsewhere and are likely to occur again. These confrontations are similar to those of police with ghetto rioters, and of police with Black Panthers; this official violence is absolved at local levels by prosecutor and grand jury (representing the white community). Prison officials are seldom chastised because the public is apathetic about prison conditions, and because American courts believe a guard's word against an inmate's and rarely probe beyond the story told by prison staff personnel.

In this case we have advanced little since the time of the Old South when slaves or free blacks could not testify in court as witnesses. The authority of prison personnel over any prison inmate is not unlike the master-slave relationship of pre–Civil War days.

RACIAL DISCRIMINATION IN PRISONS

Many prison systems in this country segregate inmates according to race and ethnic group in housing and employment because prison officials believe it will keep order, prevent racial agitation and conflict, and keep peace in the institution. Many black inmates complain that job

[3]Black Caucus of the California Assembly, *Treatment of Prisoners at California Training Facility—Soledad Central* (Sacramento, Calif.: California Legislature, 1970).

training programs are not filled by an adequate number of blacks and that certain positions for prisoners are reserved for white inmates. Blacks complain that fire department positions, clerks, runners, gas station operators, and commissary attendants are never assigned to blacks. Such jobs as cell attendants, janitors, kitchen helpers, barber shop attendants, and other low-paying, in-prison jobs are reserved primarily for black and Chicano inmates.

The judiciary does not ordinarily interfere with prison discipline, but a district court has power to grant injunctive relief when an inmate's civil rights are infringed upon by prison officers.[4]

The case of *Rivers* v. *Royster*[5] illustrates racial discrimination in prisons very clearly. Arthur L. Rivers, a black prisoner at the Virginia State Prison, brought action against M. L. Royster, assistant superintendent of the prison, under the Civil Rights Act of 1871, claiming that the prison superintendent refused him equal protection rights by denying him the right to receive a nonsubversive newspaper, the *Chicago Defender*, while permitting white inmates to receive newspapers of their choosing. Rivers was denied the *Chicago Defender* not as discipline for misconduct, but because it was a "black" newspaper.

In its review of this case, the U.S. Court of Appeals (Fourth Circuit) noted that Rivers had the right of any prisoner under Virginia law "to have and receive such newspapers and magazines as he may subscribe for or may be given to him or sent him and not deemed by the prison authorities to be subversive of discipline." Since there was no claim that the *Chicago Defender* was subversive and the censorship did not involve discipline, the alleged discrimination involved denial of a constitutional right which prevailed over the court's reluctance to interfere with prison administration and discipline. The court's ruling was that the prison superintendent may not resort to acts of racial discrimination in administering the prison.

Although courts may not interfere in cases involving racial discrimination verging on segregation, the segregation of races in prisons and jails has been held to violate the Fourteenth Amendment. In a 1966 class action against the state of Alabama, *Washington* v. *Lee*,[6] the U.S. District Court ruled that the due process and equal protection clauses of the Fourteenth Amendment protect prisoners from unconstitutional action on the part of prison authorities acting under color of state law, and that racial discrimination by government authorities in public facilities cannot be tolerated.

[4] *Sewell* v. *Pegelow*, 291 F. 2d 196 (1961).
[5] 360 F. 2d 592 (1966).
[6] 263 F. Supp. 327 (1966).

The major petitioners against racial discrimination which includes denial of religious freedom in prisons are the Black Muslims. Prison custody personnel have viewed the Black Muslims as a black-power group rather than a religious organization and claim the antiwhite posture of the Black Muslims often interfered with orderly prison management.

Because this religion is shaped by the aspirations of an important minority group, various courts scrutinized its claims of being a religion and thus deserving protection under the First Amendment. Although the Black Muslims advocate black supremacy, they deserve the freedom of other recognized religions, and their practices should be allowed in prison unless there is affirmative proof of their gross interference with prison discipline and administration.

In a 1961 case,[7] state prisoners claiming membership in the Black Muslims sought a writ of *habeas corpus* in the California Supreme Court to remove restrictions placed on them and their religious activities as Black Muslims, saying:

1. Black Muslims were not allowed a place to worship.
2. Their religious meetings were broken up, often by force.
3. They were not allowed to discuss their religious doctrines.
4. They were not allowed to possess an adequate amount of their religious literature.
5. Their religious leaders were not allowed to visit them in prison.

At that time, the California Supreme Court held that suppression of the Black Muslims as a religious group by the Director of California Corrections was not an abuse of his discretionary power to manage the California prison system.

In another 1961 case,[8] federal prisoners sought injunctive relief in the U.S. District Court (Fourth Circuit) against denial of constitutional rights because of their religion, saying they were blacks professing Islam as a faith and charging that a total of thirty-eight Black Muslims in the institution were:

1. Placed in isolation for ninety days where they were given only a teaspoon of food and a slice of bread at the three daily meal times
2. Placed in isolation cells floored with concrete, and permitted to have a blanket and mattress only from 10 P.M. to 5:30 A.M. daily
3. Deprived of institutional privileges, including medical attention

[7] *In re Ferguson*, 12 Calif. Rptr. 753 (1961).
[8] *Sewell* v. *Pegelow*, 291 F. 2d 196 (1961).

4. Forbidden to wear medals symbolic of their faith
5. Denied all opportunity to communicate with their religious advisors, recite their prayers, or receive desired religious publications.

The district court ruled that the foregoing complaints justified judicial action because their substance as a whole required a hearing for judicial examination, even if the court's action encouraged a "flood of such petitions," saying, "We must not play fast and loose with basic constitutional rights in the interest of administrative efficiency."

In 1971, a decision by the U.S. Court of Appeals (Fourth Circuit) sent a case[9] back to the district court because a prisoner of the North Carolina Central Prison brought a *pro se* (without an attorney; representing self) suit under 42 U.S.C., Section 1983, against prison authorities, claiming his constitutional right to freedom of religion was infringed because a Black Muslim minister was not admitted to the prison on the same basis as chaplains of other faiths.

CRUEL AND UNUSUAL PUNISHMENT OF PRISONERS

The Eighth Amendment forbids cruel and unusual punishment by any criminal justice agency. The burden of proof of physical mistreatment is on the injured prisoner. First, the judicial tendency not to interfere with prison discipline and administration must be overcome. Second, the resistance to believe statements of prisoners which contradict those of prison employees must be surmounted. Prison authorities usually have control of available evidence, and they pose the threat of possible retribution to other prisoner-witnesses, often effectively silencing any corroboration of the alleged physical mistreatment. The line between prison discipline and brutality is vague, and vengeance and fear often hamper the search for truth.[10]

Three important cases in the area of cruel and unusual punishment of prisoners are:

1. *Talley* v. *Stephens*, 247 F. Supp. 683 (1965), concerning physical mistreatment from beatings to "strappings" or whipping of inmates at the Arkansas State Penitentiary
2. *Jordan* v. *Fitzharris*, 257 F. Supp. 674 (1966), in which the cruel and unusual punishment was solitary confinement in a "strip" cell in the California Correctional Training Facility at Soledad, California

---

[9] *Smith* v. *Blackledge*, 451 F. 2d 1201 (1971).

[10] "Constitutional Rights of Prisoners: The Developing Law," *University of Pennsylvania Law Review*, Vol. 110 (1962), pp. 985–1008.

3. *Johnson* v. *Dye*, 175 F. 2d 250 (1949), in which the chain gangs of the Georgia prison system were exposed as places in which prisoners were victims of cruel, barbaric, and inhuman treatment at the hands of custodial personnel.

In *Talley* v. *Stephens*, the United States District Court sitting in Pine Bluff, Arkansas, did not view the whipping of prisoners by state prison employees as cruel and unusual punishment. Although the physical mistreatment in this prison could not be traced to racial discrimination in this case, the facts cited revealed that beating and whipping (blows on buttocks from a leather strap five feet in length, four inches wide, and about one-quarter inch thick, attached to a wooden handle six inches long) were at the whim of white prison employees and guards, known as "line riders" who carried firearms. In this case, one of the petitioners claimed he was beaten or whipped no less than seventy times in four years, often by his line rider, a fellow inmate convicted of murder for beating a prison employee to death.

In the Jordan case, a black prisoner was the subject of physical mistreatment, but prison authorities claimed he was not so treated because he was black, but because he was an incorrigible inmate who fought, threw objects, and used vile, abusive, and threatening language and epithets. This case reveals the physical mistreatment of one black prisoner, whether because he was black, because his conduct was beyond the reach of ordinary prison disciplinary controls, or both.

The Court commented in this case:

> When responsible prison authorities use strip cells, as in this case, they have abandoned elemental concepts of decency by permitting conditions to prevail of a shocking and debased nature, and courts must intervene promptly to restore the primal rules of a civilized community in accord with the mandate of the Constitution of the United States.

Jordan was confined in a six-by-eight-foot strip cell. The cell was constructed of solid concrete, except for a door made of bars and metal screening. The door could be covered with a metal flap to darken and silence the cell. The cell had no furnishings except a commode toilet that could not be flushed from inside the cell. (The commode was flushed twice a day by an outside guard.) Heat and ventilation were supplied by two small ducts located high in the rear wall of the cell. With the door flap down, no light or air could be admitted to the cell. Except for fifteen minutes each day, the flap was closed and the inmate remained in an airless cell in total darkness. Figures 1 and 2 show the difference between the closed cell in which Jordan was confined and the open cell which permits light, air, and noise to reach the prisoner.

Figure 1. Open cells in the Adjustment Center at San Quentin, California.

Figure 2. Closed cells in the Adjustment Center at San Quentin, California. *Photographs courtesy of the California Health and Welfare Agency, Department of Corrections.*

Jordan claimed the cell had not been cleaned for at least thirty days before he was confined to it, and it was not cleaned while he was there (twelve days). As a result of the continuous state of filth to which he was subjected, Jordan said he was often nauseous and vomited, and the vomit was never cleaned from the cell.

Jordan was forced to remain in the strip cell for twelve days without any means of cleaning his hands, body, or teeth. He had to handle and eat his food without any semblance of cleanliness or provision for sanitary conditions. For the first eight days of Jordan's confinement, he was forced to remain absolutely naked, despite the cold weather, and the cell was unheated. Thereafter, he was given only a pair of rough overalls.

He was forced to sleep on the cold concrete floor of the strip cell. A canvas mat, approximately 4½-by-5½-feet was provided, but the mat was so stiff that it could not be folded to cover him without such conscious exertion that sleep was impossible. Jordan is six feet and one inch tall.

He was denied adequate medical care before, during, and after confinement in the strip cell, despite repeated oral and written requests made in good faith by Jordan or on his behalf by other inmates. As evidence of the limited medical care provided, official records show that a doctor came into the strip cell wing only twice in the twelve days of Jordan's lock-up, spending eight minutes on one occasion and ten minutes on the other.

In *Johnson* v. *Dye*, the United States Court of Appeals (Third Circuit) held that the right to be free from cruel and unusual punishment at the hands of a state is as fundamental as the right to freedom of speech or freedom of religion. When a state officer acts illegally, the state is responsible for his acts, and the obligation of a state to treat its convicts with decency and humanity is an absolute one.

Johnson was convicted of murder in Georgia in 1942, sentenced to life imprisonment, served time in a Georgia chain gang, and escaped in 1943. He was arrested in 1946 as a fugitive in Pennsylvania, where Georgia authorities filed an executive warrant demanding Johnson's extradition and return to Georgia. In fighting extradition, Johnson claimed he was the victim of a political trial (perjured testimony by witnesses under police-prosecutor compulsion), and of cruel and unusual punishment while on the chain gang. If he returned to Georgia, he said, his life will be endangered, either by mob violence or brutal treatment by prison personnel.

The court decided it was better public policy to release Johnson, since he had received cruel and unusual punishment, and that the state of Georgia had failed in its duty to treat a convict decently and humanely.

In *Johnson*, Circuit Judge O'Connell noted in an opinion which concurred in part and dissented in part that Johnson was more than a convicted murderer in the eyes of Georgia officialdom:

> He is a Negro who has broken imprisonment and who has made virulent accusations against the white officials and guards of a Georgia public

works camp. I think it would be ingenuous to expect those Georgia authorities to accord to Johnson's constitutional rights greater respect than this court finds was conceded to Johnson during his Georgia imprisonment.

We invoke our power to release an individual who not only has suffered cruel and unusual punishment, but also faces grave and imminent danger of like abuse and very possibly even death by extra-legal means, if he is returned to Georgia.

Physical mistreatment of prisoners is often claimed to be justified or of a nature which is not cruel and unusual punishment. As late as 1970, Missouri prison officials sought to defend a prisoner's suit[11] brought under the Federal Civil Rights Act by claiming:

1. Arbitrary placement in maximum security is not cruel and unusual punishment.
2. Conditions present in such confinement are not so extreme that they constitute cruel and unusual punishment.

In this case, James L. Wilson, an inmate of the Missouri State Penitentiary at Jefferson City seeking damages and other relief, sued Lieutenant Cecil Garnett, another member of the custody division named Cook, and several other guards. In his complaint Wilson alleged he was threatened and called racist names by defendant Cook on November 6, 1969; that defendant Garnett had him committed to a seclusion cell on or about November 7, 1969, without administrative due process; that defendant Garnett sprayed him with a chemical on November 7, 1969; and that he was then placed in a small seclusion cell and forced to sleep on a concrete floor.

Fortunately, and despite the claims of Garnett and Cook that the court should not interfere with prison discipline, the court's ruling was that Wilson had a claim under the Federal Civil Rights Act suitable for judicial examination.

ACCESS TO THE COURTS—PRISONERS' RIGHTS

Access to the courts is probably the most important right of prisoners. Without court access, there is little possibility of judicial review of treatment while imprisoned and little likelihood of securing legal relief or remedy; "indefinite," erroneous convictions could never be corrected, or physical mistreatment discovered and proper action taken.

---

[11] *Wilson* v. *Garnett,* 332 F. Supp. 888 (1970).

Prison officials essentially are denying court access when they block a prisoner's attempt to communicate with a court for any length of time. Wardens have destroyed prisoners' legal petitions; custody personnel have refused to mail papers for prisoners applying to court for legal remedies; and "legal aides" have returned legal papers for rewriting solely to delay access to the court.

Another form of denying access is to forbid or to hinder the prisoner's preparation of his case for court presentation. Without books and writing materials, prisoners have no means of effective communication. Some prisons forbid legal work except at designated times and places. A prisoner's writing materials (and completed legal papers) are confiscated as "contrabrand," or the "privilege" of having them is withdrawn. Prison libraries are often not stocked with law books likely to assist prisoners in learning how to prepare legal papers and what the various routes of access to the courts for legal remedies are. In a lesser number of instances, a prisoner may be placed in solitary confinement to discourage and delay his access to the courts.

In addition, the prisoner's difficulty in obtaining access to the court cannot be redressed: if he fails to gain access he is without hope of legal relief, but if he gains access, despite delays, he no longer has a problem of access to be remedied.

In 1941, the U.S. Supreme Court held in *Ex parte Hull*[12] that a state prison rule abridging or impairing a prisoner's right to apply to the federal courts for a writ of *habeas corpus* is invalid. Cleio Hull was convicted of a sex offense in Michigan in 1936, sentenced to prison for six months to ten years, paroled in ten months, convicted in 1937 of a similar offense, and sentenced to a term of two and one-half to five years. After his second entrance into prison, he was notified that the parole board had viewed his second crime as a violation of parole, and that his new sentence on his second conviction would not begin until he had served the maximum of ten years of his first sentence.

In November, 1940, Hull prepared a petition for a writ of *habeas corpus* and exhibits. He took the papers to a prison official and requested him to notarize them. The official refused and informed the petitioner that the papers and a registered letter to the clerk of the Supreme Court concerning them would not be accepted for mailing. Hull then delivered the unnotarized papers to his father for mailing outside the prison, but guards confiscated them. Several days later, the petitioner again attempted to mail a letter concerning his case to the clerk of the Supreme Court. It was intercepted and sent to the legal investigator for the state parole board.

[12]312 U.S. 546 (1941).

About a week later Hull received the following reply from the legal investigator:

> Your letter of November 18, 1940, addressed to the Clerk of the United States Supreme Court, has been referred to the writer for reply. In the first place your application in its present form would not be acceptable to that court. You must file a petition for whatever relief you are seeking and state your reasons therefore, together with a memorandum brief. Your petition must be verified under oath and supported by proper affidavits, if any you have. Your letter was, no doubt, intercepted for the reason that it was deemed to be inadequate and which undoubtedly accounts for the fact that it found its way to my desk.

Hull then prepared another document which he somehow managed to have his father, as "agent," file with the clerk of the Supreme Court on December 26, 1940. In this document the petitioner detailed his efforts to file the papers confiscated by prison officials, contended that he was therefore unlawfully restrained, and prayed that he be released.

On January 6, 1941, the United States Supreme Court issued a ruling in which the Michigan state prison warden was directed to show cause why leave to file a petition for writ of *habeas corpus* should not be granted to *Hull*. The warden filed a return setting forth the circumstances of the two convictions, the proceedings of the parole board, and numerous exhibits. In justification of the action preventing Hull from filing his papers or communicating with the Court, the warden alleged that in November, 1940, he had published a regulation providing:

> All legal documents, briefs, petitions, motions, *habeas corpus* proceedings and appeals will first have to be submitted to the institutional welfare office and if favorably acted upon be then referred to Perry A. Maynard, legal investigator to the Parole Board, Lansing, Michigan. Documents submitted to Maynard, if in his opinion are properly drawn, will be directed to the court designated or will be referred back to the inmate.

In answer, Hull filed a "Response to the Return" challenging the validity of this regulation. The Court's ruling was that the warden's regulation was invalid; saying:

> The considerations that prompted its formulation are not without merit, but the state and its officers may not abridge or impair petitioner's right to apply to a federal court for a writ of *habeas corpus*. Whether a petition for a writ of *habeas corpus* addressed to a federal court is properly drawn and what allegations it must contain are questions for that court alone to determine.

Potential racial or ethnic discrimination lies in the power of prison personnel to deny an inmate the opportunity to prepare legal documents and to delay access to courts. Two related cases two years apart,[13] reveal the *modus operandi* of prison personnel.

In the 1959 case of *Bailleaux* v. *Holmes*, it was alleged that the defendants (prison personnel) in their official capacities had conspired to prevent the plaintiffs from exercising their constitutional rights to free and speedy court access. Plaintiffs claimed that the following restraints, among others, were unreasonable and unlawful:

1. Prisoners may not study law or prepare legal documents in their cells; they must do this work in a prison law library open only to a limited number of prisoners for limited periods of time.
2. Prisoners are severely restricted in their ability to purchase or receive law books or statutes, even though they are not available in the prison library.
3. Defendants impose special censorship on legal documents and communications with courts and attorneys.
4. Defendants confiscate legal documents found in prisoners' possession outside the library.
5. Prisoners in isolation are denied all access to the courts, counsel, and their legal papers.
6. Prisoners may not use all of their funds to purchase legal materials or pay legal fees.

In the 1961 case *Hatfield* v. *Bailleaux* the defendants (prison officials) were enjoined from:

1. Prohibiting plaintiffs not in isolation from utilizing their cell time not otherwise committed for the purpose of studying law and preparing legal documents pertaining to their respective prosecutions and legality of the judgements and sentences under which they were individually confined
2. Prohibiting plaintiffs from purchasing or receiving legal materials pertaining to their respective criminal matters, whether or not in book form and without regard to sources
3. Prohibiting plaintiffs from keeping in their respective cells their individual legal materials and legal papers pertaining to their respective criminal matters, subject to reasonable restrictions as to quantity if applicable to both legal and nonlegal materials
4. Prohibiting plaintiffs while confined to the isolation ward from communicating with or receiving communications from legal counsel or judges pertaining to their respective criminal matters

[13]*Bailleaux* v. *Holmes*, 177 F. Supp. 361 (1959); *Hatfield* v. *Bailleaux*, 290 F. 2d 632 (1961).

5. Prohibiting plaintiffs while confined to the isolation ward from having a reasonable opportunity to study legal materials and prepare legal documents pertaining to their individual criminal matters, having due regard for the purpose of isolation treatment

6. Confiscating legal documents and materials found outside specific areas designated by defendants.

POLITICAL PRISONERS

At no time in American history have social institutions been subjected to more pressures and strains than those of the present. Representatives from all minority segments of society are demanding adjustments in a network of social institutions which fails to meet their legitimate aspirations and needs.

A substantial portion of the correctional population is composed of alienated, frustrated, poor, minority adults and young persons, and the hostility, anger, and suspicion they feel is amplified by insensitive and biased correctional officials. The correctional apparatus is seen by non-white offenders as another part of an oppressive, white-dominated society, and they view themselves as political prisoners. Although the black or brown inmate is typically poor and uneducated, he has become politically knowledgeable and sensitive through his experiences.

There is a disturbing truth in the claims that this white-dominated society is using a doctrine of law and order in place of effective socioeconomic reconstruction for minorities. To be black or brown in America today is indeed a political condition, and most black and brown prisoners are at least partially the victims of polity inequity in the legal process.

Political prisoner is a term with a sociological rather than a precise legal definition. Legally, it refers to someone who is prosecuted or jailed for harboring or expressing opinions antagonistic to established government, but treason or advocating the forcible overthrow of government is not often charged in the courts of this country. Therefore, *political prisoner* actually describes persons who would not be in prison if they were not unfairly discriminated against.

An example of such a prisoner is California's George Jackson, who was sentenced to prison at nineteen years of age for a seventy-dollar robbery for which a white youth of nineteen would have possibly received probation or commitment to the Youth Authority. Jackson believed that he was a political prisoner since he was imprisoned for a petty robbery, that he was placed in solitary confinement for his political beliefs and verbal attacks on the prison system, and that continual denial of his parole was based on the same factors.[14]

In George Jackson's view, the relationship between prison authorities and black inmates is that of the keeper and the kept and involves much political and ideological antagonism. He believes these attitudes result from a reaction to the black politicizing in ghettos and efforts of prison inmates to unite along racial lines despite their virtual segregation in prison blocks and cell tiers.

In 1971, the population in the state prison at Attica, New York, was close to 2000 men. Eighty-five percent were black or brown. They seized hostages and made demands on the prison officials. In the confrontation pattern common to all prison riots, the inmate leaders of this rebellion warned prison officials: "We know you can play games, but you are not going to play games and find any hostages alive. Mind you, we are ready to die." Forty-two men were killed, ten of them hostages, when state police armed with rifles and shotguns put down the revolt in the fifth day of the riot.

This riot was the reaction of political prisoners to the oppressive weight of the white-dominated prison organization and an attempt to demonstrate the resulting despair on the part of blacks and browns who cannot hope to gain their freedom. The political prisoner is one who failed to abide by the law because of the psychological and social damage of social discrimination and segregation in ghettos. He believes he is being physically mistreated and denied legal remedies while imprisoned because of race or ethnic origin. He may also feel he was not accorded due process of the law and equal treatment when arrested, convicted, and sentenced.

The political prisoner is an inmate who knows he was rejected for probation because his resources as a black or brown were not equal to those of the whites, and who knows he is going to a prison where the correctional officer's word against a minority inmate's is rarely questioned, where the "due process" of prison disciplinary hearings denies him the right to confront accusers and to cross-examine them, and in which he may be penalized by:

1. Loss of "good" time
2. Imposition of additional years of imprisonment by denial of parole release
3. Transfer to another prison
4. Loss of privileges

[14]Jackson spent seven out of eleven years in various adjustment centers in solitary confinement.

5. Confinement to segregation
6. Denial of medical care
7. Loss of job or study assignment
8. Discriminatory work assignment
9. Whipping or other physical mistreatment.

JUDICIAL MURDER AND THE DEATH PENALTY

Judicial murder is the only term that adequately signifies the inherent injustice of death sentences meted out as the result of biased political trials or to persons convicted because of a class distinction rather than an individual crime.

In the last years of Charles II's reign as monarch of England and the early reign of James, the English judiciary, under Lord Chief Justice Jeffreys, sent hundreds of men to their deaths in the pseudotrials that followed a feeble and stupid attempt to seize the throne. When the ordeal ended, scores had been executed and 1,200 were awaiting the hangman in three counties. To be absent from home during the uprising was evidence of guilt. Death was considered too mild for the villagers and farmers rounded up in these raids; the directions to a high sheriff were to provide an ax, a cleaver, a furnace or cauldron to boil their heads and quarters, and soil to boil therewith, half a bushel to each traitor, and tar to tar them with, and a sufficient number of spears and poles to fix their heads and quarters along the highways.

The story of these political trials, known as the Bloody Assizes, was widely known to the framers of the United States Constitution. Although the hundreds of judicial murders committed by Jeffreys and his fellow judges are totally inconceivable in a free American republic, the legal rulings that permitted the murders could easily be used against any person whose political opinions challenged the party in power if the United States Constitution did not forbid cruel and unusual punishment.

It is, no doubt, harsh and unusual to relate these former judicial murders in England to the death penalty in America at this time, but attorneys and criminologists have agreed for many years that only the poor, the mentally ill, the ignorant, the powerless, or the hated have been executed under judicial death sentences. Blacks have been executed not only for murder, but also for lesser crimes such as rape.

Recently, the United States Supreme Court accepted three cases in which the death penalty had been imposed; the convicted persons were all black.[15] This judicial review revealed in full, for the first time, the potential for sentencing black persons convicted of murder or rape to death mainly because they were black; it revealed a system of law and justice that leaves to the uncontrolled discretion of judges and juries the decision whether a convicted defendant should die or be imprisoned.

In *Furman* v. *Georgia* and two companion cases, the Supreme Court ruled directly for the first time on the constitutionality of capital punishment under the Eighth Amendment's cruel and unusual punishment clause. Each of the three petitioners had been sentenced to death, and in each case the decision to impose the death penalty had been left to a jury. The question presented in these cases is whether death is a "cruel and unusual" punishment and thus, by virtue of the Eighth and Fourteenth Amendments, beyond the power of the state to inflict. The Court held, in a 5–4 *per curiam* opinion, that the imposition of the death penalty in these cases constitutes cruel and unusual punishment in violation of the Eighth and Fourteenth Amendments.

The circumstances of the three cases of petitioners Jackson, Furman, and Branch are:

1. *Jackson,* a black convicted of the rape of a white woman, was twenty-one years old. A court-appointed psychiatrist said that Jackson was of average education and intelligence, that he was not imbecilic, schizophrenic, or psychotic, that his traits were the product of environmental influences, and that he was competent to stand trial. Jackson had entered the house after the husband left for work. He held scissors against the neck of the wife, demanding money. She could find none and a struggle ensued for the scissors. She was then raped while Jackson kept the scissors pressed against her neck. While there did not appear to be any long-term traumatic impact on the victim, she was bruised and abrased in the struggle but was not hospitalized. Jackson was a convict who had escaped from a work gang in the area, a result of a three-year sentence for auto theft. He was at large for three days and during that time had committed several other offenses: burglary, auto theft, and assault and battery.

2. *Furman,* a black, killed a householder while seeking to enter a home at night. Furman fired the shot through a closed door. He was twenty-six years old and had finished the sixth grade. Pending trial he was committed to the Georgia Central State Hospital for a psychiatric examination on his plea of insanity tendered by court-appointed counsel. The superintendent reported a staff diagnostic conference on the same date had concluded that "this patient should retain his present diagnosis of mental deficiency, mild to moderate, with psychotic episodes associated with

---

[15]*Furman* v. *Georgia*, 408 U.S. 238 (1972), along with *Jackson* v. *Georgia,* and *Branch* v. *Texas.*

convulsive disorder." The physicians agreed that "at present the patient is not psychotic, but he is not capable of cooperating with his counsel in the preparation of his defense," and that the staff believed that "he is in need of further psychiatric hospitalization and treatment."

3. *Branch*, a black, entered the rural home of a sixty-five-year-old white widow while she slept and raped her, holding his arm against her throat. He then demanded money and she searched for thirty minutes or more, finding little. As he left, Branch said if the widow told anyone what had happened, he would return and kill her. The record is barren of any medical or psychiatric evidence showing injury to her as a result of Branch's attack.

Branch had previously been convicted of felony theft and found to be a borderline mentally deficient, well below the average intelligence quotient of Texan prison inmates. He had the equivalent of five and a half years of grade school education and was in the lower four percent of his class.

Each of the five concurring justices filed a separate opinion. Justices Douglas, Stewart, and White each relied on the fact that the death sentences in these cases were not mandatorily imposed by the legislature for the particular crime but were imposed at the discretion of the jury. Justice Douglas argued that the statutes before the Court allowed judges or juries to apply the death penalty selectively:

In a nation committed to equal protection of the laws there is no permissible "caste" aspect of law enforcement. Yet we know that the discretion of judges and juries in imposing the death penalty enables the penalty to be selectively applied, feeding prejudices against the accused if he is poor and despised, poor and lacking political clout, or if he is a member of a suspect or unpopular minority, and saving those who by social position may be in a more protected position. In ancient Hindu law a Brahmin was exempt from capital punishment. And in those days, generally, in the law books, punishment increased in severity, as social status diminished. We have, I fear, taken in practice the same position, partially as a result of making the death penalty discretionary and partially as a result of the ability of the rich to purchase the services of the most respected and most resourceful legal talent in the nation.

The high service rendered by the "cruel and unusual" punishment clause of the Eighth Amendment is to require legislatures to write penal laws that are even-handed, nonselective, and nonarbitrary, and to require judges to see to it that general laws are not applied sparsely, selectively and spottily to unpopular groups.

A law that stated that anyone making more than $50,000 would be exempt from the death penalty would plainly fall, as would a law that in [similar] terms said that blacks, those who never went beyond the fifth grade in school, or those who made less than $3,000 a year, or those who were unpopular or unstable should be the only people executed. A law which in the overall view reaches that result in practice has no more sanctity than a law which in terms provides the same.

Thus, these discretionary statutes are unconstitutional in their operation. They are pregnant with discrimination, and discrimination is an ingredient not compatible with the idea of equal protection of the laws that is implicit in the ban on "cruel and unusual" punishments.

Justice Douglas found this mandate of equal treatment in the cruel and unusual punishment clause of the English Bill of Rights, the source of the American version. Historically, he argued, the clause was a reaction not only to barbaric punishments, but also to the selective and irregular imposition of penalties upon persons disfavored by the British crown. The clause is similarly applicable, the justice argued, to the selective and irregular imposition of the death penalty upon socially disfavored persons in America today. The concluding paragraph of this segment of his opinion reads:

> Those who wrote the Eighth Amendment knew what price their forebears had paid for a system based, not on equal justice, but on discrimination. In those days the target was not the blacks or the poor, but the dissenters, those who opposed absolutism in government, who struggled for a parliamentary regime, and who opposed government's recurring efforts to foist a particular religion on the people. But the tool of capital punishment was used with vengeance against the opposition and those unpopular with the regime. One cannot read this history [English] without realizing that the desire for equality was reflected in the ban against "cruel and unusual" punishment contained in the Eighth Amendment.

Throughout the sparse case histories of these three cases, there is an apparent politicalization of the defendants. Each case contains a record of imprisonment, and the locale of incarceration strongly implies discrimination and physical mistreatment. Further, there are strong implications that the defendants were political prisoners as they appeared to be products of their environment: the low quality of separate-but-equal education, and the failure to diagnose and treat persons who may be mentally ill at the time of the commission of a crime. Lastly, Furman, Jackson, and Branch can be classed as political prisoners because they were sentenced to death at the whim of a judge or jury who acted not in accord with stated standards but in accord with motives as likely to emanate from their own experiences in Texas and Georgia as from the evidence presented in each case.

DISCUSSION QUESTIONS

1. What are the common forms of racial discrimination in prison?
2. Assess the circumstances of the Soledad killings. What conduct by correctional personnel is implied by these facts?
3. How are the routes to court access blocked by prison officials?
4. What is a political prisoner?
5. What facts support the claim that the last fifty years of the death penalty in the United States qualify as judicial murder?

CASE REFERENCES

Bailleaux v. *Holmes*, 177 F. Supp. 361 (1959).

Furman v. *Georgia*, 408 U.S. 238 (1972), along with *Jackson* v. *Georgia*, and *Branch* v. *Texas*.

Hatfield v. *Bailleaux*, 290 F. 2d 632 (1961).

Johnson v. *Dye*, 175 F. 2d 250 (1949).

Jordan v. *Fitzharris*, 257 F. Supp. 674 (1966).

Rivers v. *Royster*, 360 F. 2d 592 (1966).

Sewell v. *Pegelow*, 291 F. 2d 196 (1961).

Smith v. *Blackledge*, 451 F. 2d 1201 (1971).

Talley v. *Stephens*, 247 F. Supp. 683 (1965).

Washington v. *Lee*, 263 F. Supp. 327 (1966).

Wilson v. *Garnett*, 332 F. Supp. 888 (1970).

7

Standards for
Equal Treatment
of Minorities

DUE PROCESS FOR PRISONERS AND PAROLEES
POLICE FIELD INTERROGATION AND STOP-AND-FRISK
PREVENTION OF PHYSICAL MISTREATMENT
  OF SUSPECTS AND PRISONERS
CONTROL OF OFFICIAL VIOLENCE—FIREARMS
POLICE SURVEILLANCE OF POLITICAL ACTIVITIES
GRAND JURIES
TRIAL JURIES AND MINORITY DEFENDANTS
RELEASE OF MINORITY ARRESTEES ON BAIL
FAIR TRIAL

Discrimination in Johannesburg, South Africa, may be worse than that in the southern ghettos and barrios of the United States, but such use of discrimination elsewhere to preserve some form of a caste system does not justify its continued use in this country. The treatment of southern blacks, the brown people of the Southwest, and the New York Puerto Ricans concerns every American. People of the United States should reexamine the meaning of freedom and equality and acknowledge that the increasing bitterness and hostility of disadvantaged minorities are a direct result of white domination and discrimination. An inexorable law of human nature is that one cannot deny the humanity of another person without diminishing one's own.[1]

If minorities are to receive the equal justice and protection guaranteed to all United States citizens by the Constitution in general, and the Fourteenth Amendment in particular, minimum standards for behavior of criminal justice agents toward all people should be established. Because police, prosecutor, judiciary, juries, and correctional personnel have a vast amount of power over people's present and future lives, their official actions must conform to standards of equitable and unbiased treatment of all men regardless of racial or national background. Recommendations follow which suggest standards to fit the framework of existing statute and case law.

DUE PROCESS FOR PRISONERS AND PAROLEES

The due process protection of the Fourteenth Amendment is flexible and calls for such procedural protections as the particular situation demands. When the situation is that of a convicted person on probation, prisoner, or parolee, the circumstances of grievous loss of liberty and physical mistreatment warrant a hearing in which due process is assured by procedural safeguards.

The politicalization of persons convicted of crime may be lessened if the white-dominated courts and society accept implementation at realistic levels of the constitutional guarantee of due process and are willing to help all political prisoners gain the procedural safeguards of due process. These safeguards are necessary—

1. when disciplinary action, such as solitary confinement or loss of "good" time, which serves to increase actual term of imprisonment, is taken against a prisoner;
2. when a maximum sentence is set as a result of action by an extrajudicial body (such as Adult Authority or Parole Board), and years are added to the sentence without the privilege of freedom on the basis of behavior in prison;
3. when the issue is whether or not parole should be revoked and the parolee returned to prison, or whether or not probation should be revoked and the offender committed to prison;
4. when the issue is whether any person on probation, in prison, or on parole has been denied access to court in seeking a legal remedy aligned with his status as a convicted criminal defendant.

[1]James Baldwin, *Nobody Knows My Name* (New York: Dial Press, 1961), pp. 68–71.

When convicted black or brown persons protest against the unfairness of revoked probation and commitment to prison, of discrimination and physical mistreatment in prison, or of delay in parole release or parole revocation on the basis of their race or skin color, the hearing on the complaint is usually no more than a summary review conducted by the person complained about or associated with that person as fellow probation, prison, or parole employees. In effect, as with grievances against police by citizens, it is a case of employees being investigated by their fellow employees who are likely to side with them.

The Court gave a detailed prescription in *Morrissey* v. *Brewer*[2] for minimum procedural safeguards required by due process when a state seeks to revoke parole. Petitioner Morrissey was arrested at the direction of his parole officer and held as a parole violator. Shortly afterwards, he was recommitted to prison by the Iowa Board of Parole, acting on the parole officers' recommendations. On the record before the Court, Morrissey was not given a hearing at the time of his arrest or when the board revoked his parole. These omissions were held by the Court to have deprived the petitioner of due process.

In this case, the Court ruled that parole was not a privilege to be dispensed or withdrawn at the whim of a state agent and that freedom on parole had a basic value to a parolee which justifies invoking the due process protection of the Fourteenth Amendment to guard against arbitrary and discriminatory action.

The Court in *Morrissey* v. *Brewer* described the features of an acceptable hearing. Soon after a parolee has been arrested, "someone not directly involved in the case" must conduct a "minimum inquiry" near the place of arrest or alleged parole violation. The presiding officer must compile an informal record of the proceedings and decide, stating reasons, whether there is probable cause to believe that the parolee has violated parole conditions and, if so, whether the violations justify his reincarceration. Conclusions on these questions must be expressed in a written, reasoned statement. At both the preliminary inquiry and the revocation hearing, a parolee is entitled to receive notice of the charges against him, to confront adverse witnesses, to speak, and to present his own witnesses and evidence.

While the Court explicitly refused to decide in *Morrissey* whether a parolee must be permitted to retain counsel, or whether counsel must be appointed for an indigent, the loss-of-liberty factor implies that the Sixth Amendment guarantee of the right to legal assistance is applicable. Also unresolved in the procedural safeguards in this case was the burden and standard of proof. Again, the loss-of-liberty factor implies

[2]408 U.S. 471 (1972).

that the burden of proof of guilt is on the state, and that the standard of evidence should be no less than proof beyond a reasonable doubt.

Recommendation: To provide effective action that will protect black and brown prisoners and parolees from discrimination by state agents, the procedural safeguards of the *Morrissey* v. *Brewer* case should be formalized at all disciplinary hearings which could place an inmate in solitary confinement, cut "good" time, lengthen an indeterminate sentence, or revoke parole. Legal counsel should be allowed and indigent prisoners or parolees provided with funds to hire counsel of their own choosing. The burden of proving "guilt" (misconduct or forbidden behavior) should rest with the state; the standard of proof is proof beyond a reasonable doubt. Details of the hearing should be "on the record."

POLICE FIELD INTERROGATION AND STOP-AND-FRISK

There is no formal legal authorization which sanctions field interrogation (FI) in the absence of an actual arrest. But in many jurisdictions, the police have conducted field interrogations and the judiciary has tacitly supported them. For years, police patrol officers have been stopping suspicious persons on foot or in vehicles and inquiring about their identity and the nature of their presence in various areas. Police believe that the practice is essential to prevent crime and to apprehend offenders.

Police field interrogation has become a prime public issue because patrol officers have been accused of indiscriminately stopping and frisking persons. Some police forces routinely search known criminals, shabbily dressed persons, or minority group members. Some police field interrogations are conducted primarily in slum communities, where persons may be questioned indiscriminately rather than for objective reasons, and where some patrolmen have asked questions in an unfriendly and abusive fashion. As a result, field interrogations are a major source of friction between police and minority group members. In addition, the efficacy of field interrogations has become an issue, especially in highly urbanized areas.[3]

Police stop-and-frisk activity may precede or follow field interrogation. In *Terry* v. *Ohio,*[4] the United States Supreme Court recognized the concept of stopping and frisking persons suspected of criminal activity, even though the observed circumstances at the time were less

---

[3]George D. Eastman and Esther M. Eastman, eds., *Municipal Police Administration,* 6th ed. (Washington, D.C.: International City Management Association, 1969), p. 92.

[4]392 U.S. 1 (1968).

than probable cause to arrest, if the officer feared the person carried weapons. In this decision the U.S. Supreme Court did not retreat from its position that police should generally seek warrants from the judiciary to authorize searches and seizures but set up procedural safeguards which would protect the privacy of citizens from police searches without prior judicial approval. The abuse of this authority derived from *Terry* has become a problem in ghettos and *barrios.*

Now that the *Terry* doctrine has been extended by *Adams* v. *Williams,*[5] the problem may have new dimensions. The circumstances of *Adams* v. *Williams* and the brief majority opinion written by Justice Rehnquist are:

> *Circumstances:* Acting on a tip supplied moments earlier by an informant known to him, a police officer, Sgt. John Connolly, asked respondent Williams to open his car door. Williams lowered the window, and Connolly reached into the car and found a loaded handgun (which had not been visible from the outside) in Williams' waistband, precisely where the informant said it would be. Williams was arrested for unlawful possession of the handgun. A search incident to the arrest disclosed heroin on Williams' person (as the informant had reported), as well as other contraband in the car. Williams' petition for federal *habeas corpus* relief was denied by the U.S. District Court. The U.S. Court of Appeals reversed, holding that the evidence that had been used in the trial resulting in respondent's conviction had been obtained by an unlawful search.
>
> As *Terry* v. *Ohio,* 392 U.S. 1, recognizes, a policeman making a reasonable investigatory stop may conduct a limited protective search for concealed weapons when he has reason to believe that the suspect is armed and dangerous. Here the information from the informant had enough indicia of reliability to justify the officer's forcible stop of petitioner and the protective seizure of the weapon, which afforded reasonable ground for the search incident to the arrest that ensued.

Terry did not hold that whenever a policeman suspects a citizen of engaging in criminal activity he may engage in a stop and frisk. It held that if police officers want to stop and frisk they must have specific facts from which they can reasonably infer that an individual is engaged in criminal activity and is armed and dangerous.[6] It was central to the Court's decision in *Terry* that the police officer acted on the basis of his own personal observations and that he carefully scrutinized the suspects' conduct before interfering with them in any way.

As a result of the Court's decision in *Adams,* the balance struck in *Terry* is now heavily weighed in favor of the government. This imbal-

[5] 407 U.S. 143 (1972).
[6] *Terry* v. *Ohio,* p. 29; *Sibron* v. *New York,* 393 U.S., p. 64.

ance is a serious contradiction of the Fourth Amendment, which was included in the Bill of Rights to prevent arbitrary and oppressive police action. The decision in *Adams* invokes the spectre of a society in which innocent citizens may be stopped, searched, and arrested at the whim of police officers who have only the slightest suspicion of improper conduct.

Recommendation: To protect minorities against harassment and unfair application of the doctrine of *Adams,* police field interrogations should be limited to situations which authorize the stop-and-frisk procedure of *Terry:* observation by a police officer which, along with his police expertise, provide objective reasons as cause for the stop, and no more than a superficial protective search for weapons if the circumstances make the officer fear the suspect has weapons and may use them to injure the officer. No information regarding the identity of the person stopped should be placed in the criminal records of the police department or sheriff's office unless the person can be connected with a crime under investigation.

PREVENTION OF PHYSICAL MISTREATMENT OF SUSPECTS AND PRISONERS

Because prison walls conceal inmates' complaints regarding physical mistreatment, particularly the use of Mace and tear gas, from the public, police use of unnecessary force appears to be a prevalent practice. Whether police "brutality" exceeds prison personnel "physical mistreatment" of inmates is a moot point. Both practices should be abolished by establishing impartial tribunals at less-than-court levels where the complaints will be given a fair hearing on their merits.

Traditionally, the question, Who watches the watchmen?, has always been a problem. Complainants are forced to present their grievances to the employing agency, with the result that police investigate allegations of police misconduct, and correctional officers' alleged misbehavior is investigated by their prison supervisors or associates. It is little wonder that this Alice-in-Wonderland procedure rejects most complaints as unfounded.

If a complainant remains dissatisfied with the disposition of a case, other avenues of appeal outside the employing agency exist: the local prosecutor; the courts; elected officials such as councilmen or mayor; the State's attorney general; and the U.S. Department of Justice. Other forums exist in some jurisdictions, such as civilian review boards.

Although some kinds of official conduct have traditionally been subject to review by the courts, it is very difficult to determine the impact of this review. It seems likely, however, that judicial influence has not been substantial except where the exclusionary rule has been applied. Many forms of official misconduct are not violations of the criminal law, and, when the law is broken, action is limited by the problem of proof and credibility of testimony. In many cases, the only witnesses to the misconduct are the police or correctional officer and the victim, and often the victim and any nonpolice witnesses are from minority groups and have criminal records. In addition, many prosecutors are reluctant to bring charges except in serious cases because they work so closely with the police.

Civil cases also have serious difficulties. The chief witnesses are still likely to be the alleged victim and the police or correctional officer. Even if a victim is successful in the case, the officer may not be able to pay the judgement. Unless the prospect of payment is substantial, there is little incentive for the victim to incur the costs of investigation and counsel necessary to the suit or for counsel to take the case on a contingent fee basis. In many jurisdictions, the alternative of suit against the employing agency is blocked by the doctrine of sovereign immunity, and it is often not clear whether the governmental agency is liable for nonnegligent misconduct.

The principal federal criminal statute relating to such misconduct is Section 242 of Title 18 which prohibits the deprivation "under the color of any law . . . of any rights, privileges or immunities secured or protected by the Constitution or laws of the United States . . . on account of such inhabitant being an alien or by reason of his color or race." The principal federal civil statute, 42 U.S.C. 1983, is almost identical to the federal criminal statute. It covers excessive force, arrest without probable cause, illegal searches, and other violations of constitutional rights and provides for injunctions as well as money damages.

In the area of police brutality, many citizens, particularly those from minority groups and civil rights organizations, have been dissatisfied with police internal review procedures. They urge the creation of civilian review boards to investigate and determine the validity of citizen complaints. Civilian review boards of one sort or another were established in Washington, D.C. (1948), Philadelphia (1958), Minneapolis and York, Pennsylvania (1960), Rochester (1963), and New York City (1966). Boards have been proposed in many other cities, including Chicago, Cincinnati, Detroit, Los Angeles, Oakland, Newark, Pittsburgh, and Seattle. Bills have been introduced in the California, Massachusetts, and New York legislatures to require large cities or the state to form such boards.

But civilian review boards have had a stormy history. The boards in Philadelphia and Rochester have been the subject of court suits with injunctions against their operation during part of their existence. The board in Washington, D.C., was severely criticized for inaction and was thoroughly reorganized in 1965. The boards in Minneapolis and York never actually operated. The board in New York City, after a very heated political campaign, was rejected by the electorate and has been replaced by a board composed of civilian police employees. While the boards which have gone into operation have differed somewhat in organization and details, their basic concept has been the same; they have been advisory only, having no power to decide cases. The New York City and Washington, D.C., boards have even lacked the power to indicate their views on the merits of the case and are limited to recommending whether a police trial was necessary or not.[7]

While the police have rejected civilian review boards as an external review of professional activities, the Black Panthers reject them as within the "fascist power structure" and no more than a civilian front to continue the police control of police.[8]

Prison and police organizations resist change. Payment of damages and the cost of legal defense are often borne by police and correctional officer associations. Litigation should not be the only means of overseeing police behavior, and the uselessness of the rule suggested by the President's Commission on Law Enforcement and Administration of Justice is apparent in its vagueness: "Every jurisdiction should provide adequate procedures for full and fair processing of all citizen grievances and complaints about the conduct of any public officer or employee."[9]

A democratic government should require police and prison officials to justify and explain the actions of their subordinates.

Recommendation: Police should no longer investigate police, nor prison officials investigate correctional officers, when complaints are made charging police brutality or physical mistreatment of prisoners. Organizations representing minorities should establish review boards to examine the merit of complaints and to maintain an account indicating the cumulative and continuing nature of such conduct. Class actions should be prepared against police or prison officials who fail to prevent such conduct by subordinates. Further, the cost of such review, accounting, and legal preparation when warranted should be a charge against the employing agency (just as is the cost of their present ineffec-

[7]President's Commission on Law Enforcement and Administration of Justice, *Task Force Report: The Police* (Washington, D.C.: U.S. Government Printing Office, 1967), p. 200.

[8]Bobby Seale, *Seize the Time: The Story of the Black Panther Party and Huey P. Newton* (New York: Random House, 1968), p. 421.

[9]*Task Force Report: Police*, p. 103.

tive internal investigation of complaints), and federal legislation should be initiated to make prompt satisfaction of such claims a prerequisite to federal funding of the employing agency (just as federal legislation has made the failure of certain public employers to follow rules for reasonable "affirmative action" in hiring minorities the cause for witholding federal funds).

CONTROL OF OFFICIAL VIOLENCE—FIREARMS

Both preventive and punitive action is needed to prevent unnecessary official violence and the great harm caused by firearms used in such situations. Throughout the United States, local jurisdictions have laws justifying the necessary use of force by police officers and outlining the instances in which officials can be absolved should death occur as the result of necessary force. Legal justification is denied to the police officer, however, whenever it is determined that the force used may have been disproportionate to the situation or provocation, or if the officer should have foreseen that injuries were likely to result from his actions.

Although police may be exonerated from criminal liability in homicides, a civil suit against an officer may be based on negligence arising from the circumstances of the homicide, and damages will be awarded to the plaintiff if it can be shown that the police officer failed to use reasonable care.

In a Florida police shooting in which a bystander was killed at the scene of a police-black confrontation in one of Miami's ghetto areas, the Florida Supreme Court ruled that there was strong evidence that the shooting occurred as an overreaction to possible sniper fire. The court affirmed the trial jury's verdict that the police had acted unreasonably according to the facts presented in this case: a 10- to 15-second barrage of 75 to 100 shots fired into a crowd of black residents in front of, and on the steps and balconies of a 3-story public housing facility in Miami.[10]

Whether there was an unlawful, riotous, or tumultuous assembly was an evidentiary question in this case. There was considerable evidence that the killing was not necessary to disperse a crowd, nor did it occur when a member of the crowd who had refused to disperse was being arrested. The police were standing on a vacant lot watching a building whose lighted balconies were filled with men, women, and children. The only arrest had been made earlier before all the police cars arrived. The testimony conflicts on whether or not the people on the balconies

---

[10] *Cleveland* v. *Miami (City of) Florida,* 263 So. 2d 573 (1972).

had heard an earlier request to return to their apartments. At the time of the shooting, things appeared quiet; at least one patrol car had already left the scene.

In this decision the majority of the Florida Supreme Court approved the trial judge's ruling that Florida law exonerating policemen in the use of reasonable force at such assemblies did not *ipso facto* settle the evidentiary question of negligence and permitted the jury to decide that factual issue.

Recommendation: Federal legislation should be initiated which will require a written firearms policy in all police departments in the United States to class police firearms as weapons of defense, not offense. Such a law would place responsibility on the federal prosecutory complex for appropriate action in police shooting cases in which minorities sustain injury or death and when local action appears to whitewash the shooting.

POLICE SURVEILLANCE OF POLITICAL ACTIVITIES

Police surveillance of political activities by minorities in ghettos and *barrios* discourages exercise of the First Amendment right to free expression. Police officials say that such surveillance is necessary to obtain information on potential disruptions and that it helps police prevent crime, suppress riots, and keep order. Black Muslims and Black Panthers, the Brown Berets and other Chicano organizations, and the Puerto Rico Nationalists say that police often misuse the information collected as a result of such surveillances and that their exercise of First Amendment rights is inhibited by the knowledge that their activities are watched by police.

Police surveillance of the political activities of disadvantaged minorities has been linked to suspected criminal activity as justification for raids, searches, and seizures.

There is now little doubt that the FBI wiretapped Dr. Martin Luther King's telephone conversations; that the armed forces of the country have been employed in surveillances of citizens; that much of the collected and often unevaluated data is passed on to police "intelligence" units for their uninhibited use and possibly to encourage similar surveillance activity.

In the 1972 case *Laird* v. *Tatum*,[11] the United States Supreme Court rejected the claim that United States Army surveillance of political activities in itself constituted a discouragement of First Amendment

[11]408 U.S. 1 (1972).

rights, but the circumstances of the case and the content of the various opinions in *Tatum* exposed the scope of such surveillance and its threat to privacy.

The plaintiffs in *Tatum* were civilians whose lawful political activities protesting government policies were subjected to surveillance by army intelligence. They sought declaratory and injunctive relief in federal district court against such army activity. The army explained that such surveillance was necessary to obtain information on potential disruptions so that the military might, without applying "blind force," fulfill its statutory obligation of suppressing domestic insurrection when called on to do so by the president. Whenever there is an insurrection in any state against its government, the president, upon the request of the state's legislature or its governor if the legislature cannot be convened, may call into federal service the militia of other states in the number requested by that state, and use the armed forces as he considers necessary to suppress the insurrection.

The district court dismissed the case on the ground that such an injury was too speculative. A divided panel of the United States Court of Appeals for the District of Columbia reversed that decision, holding that since the complaint alleged that *existing* army intelligence activities restricted the *present* exercise of First Amendment rights, the claim was sufficiently concrete to be justifiable. In an opinion by Chief Justice Burger, the Supreme Court reversed the decision, 5–4.

The Court's decision in *Tatum* was surprising because it was the first time the Court demanded that a suit alleging infringement of First Amendment rights be based on an existing inhibition or threat of a specific future inhibition of these rights.

Justice Douglas dissented in an opinion joined by Justice Marshall. The concluding paragraphs of the Douglas dissent sum up the hazard of military surveillance of civilian citizens:

> This case is a cancer in our body politic. It is a measure of the disease which afflicts us. Army surveillance, like Army regimentation, is at war with the principles of the First Amendment. Those who already walk submissively will say there is no cause for alarm. But submissiveness is not our heritage. The First Amendment was designed to allow rebellion to remain as our heritage. The Constitution was designed to keep government off the backs of the people. The Bill of Rights was added to keep the precepts of belief and expression, of the press, of political and social activities free from surveillance.
>
> The Bill of Rights was designed to keep agents of government and official eavesdroppers away from the people. The aim was to allow men to be free and independent and to assert their rights against government. There can be no influence more paralyzing of that objective than Army

surveillance. When an Intelligence Officer looks over every nonconformist's shoulder in the library or walks invisibly by his side in a picket line or infiltrates his club, the America once extolled as the voice of liberty heard around the world no longer is cast in the image which Jefferson and Madison designed, but more in the Russian image.[12]

There is no doubt that if the word "police" were substituted for "army" in the above case, the discussion of First Amendment freedoms in jeopardy because of surveillance of political activities would also apply to the harassment by police of minority-group organizations in ghettos and *barrios*.

Recommendation: Persons aggrieved by police surveillance in ghettos and *barrios* should have the power to seek a large-scale investigation conducted by themselves as private parties armed with the subpoena power of a federal district court and the power of cross-examination to probe into the police intelligence-gathering activities. The United States District Court of local jurisdiction could determine at the conclusion of the investigation the extent to which those activities are appropriate to the police mission by hearing evidence, ascertaining the facts, and deciding what, if any, further restrictions on the activities complained about are called for to confine the police to their legitimate sphere of activity and to protect infringed constitutional rights.

This recommendation reflects only the traditional resistance of Americans to any police intrusion into civilian affairs. The roots of that tradition are found in the Third Amendment's explicit prohibition against quartering soldiers in private homes without consent and in the constitutional provisions for civilian control of the military. This recommendation also reflects the fear of pervasive growth of any secret police unit until a malignant condition develops. No other growth process could describe the approval in 1970 of the most wide-ranging secret police operation ever authorized in the peacetime United States, a cooperative effort by the nation's most powerful intelligence agencies: the FBI, Central Intelligence Agency (CIA), National Security Agency (NSA), and Defense Intelligence Agency (DIA). This operation included "intelligence gathering" by bugging, burglary, and blackmail by government agents against American citizens, antiwar activists, campus radicals and militant Black Panthers, foreign students and diplomats. One proposal would have created a new cadre of "super-secret agents" for domestic missions whose operations could not be traced to any federal agency and whose identity and assignments would be concealed from all but the highest agency officials. The justification for this super-secret police was that national security had to be protected by whatever

[12] *Laird* v. *Tatum*, 408 U.S. 1 (1972).

means necessary. This domestic spying, however, was planned to do more than inhibit activities of those subject to its technology; it was planned as a deliberate, widespread, and clandestine repression of civil liberties.[13]

In 1973, the foregoing plan was termed "dead" and "inoperative" after public exposure, but the frightening aspect of the plan was the philosophy of the federal government in using an end-justifies-the-means doctrine against its own dissenting citizens.

GRAND JURIES

Historically, the function of the grand jury was to protect the individual accused of crime from unfair treatment by prosecuting officials. In reality, grand juries show little concern for protecting the individual from wrongful prosecution. The folklore of our American legal system holds that grand juries are comprised of individuals of high and low estate, from all vocational backgrounds (except law enforcement), and represent a "cross section" of the community. In reality, grand jurors are selected from among the elite in the community, white and well-to-do, and possibly Protestant; minorities and poor people are omitted.

Competence to serve as a grand juror is an individual rather than a group or class matter, and representatives of every stratum of society likely to be encompassed in a fair cross section of a community can be found who are eligible and competent to serve on a grand jury. A fair cross section of the community will be represented on grand juries only when the juror selection process ensures there is no underrepresentation of any economic or racial group.

At one time, daily wage laborers were systematically excluded from grand jury panels because jury commissioners believed that such persons wanted to be excused for reasons of hardship. The exclusion of daily wage earners as a class violated the due process and equal protection rights to an impartial jury representing a fair cross section of the community. Of course, jury duty is a burden on persons of low economic status, but this segment of the community is so large and so important to a fair hearing for accused persons similarly situated that a jury system without daily wage earners is not representative of the community. As it can be rectified by night hearing sessions and a reduction in the grand jury's work load, this exclusion is no longer excusable.

Unlike trial jurors, grand jurors are not examined on *voir dire* to determine their qualifications, or possible bias or prejudice, and defense attorneys in cases processed before a grand jury do not have any per-

[13]"Blueprint for a Super Secret Police," *Newsweek*, 4 June 1973. pp. 18–19.

emptory challenges to dismiss a prospective grand juror suspected of bias or prejudice.

Hearings before grand juries, unlike criminal court trials, are not based on our adversarial legal system. They are *ex parte* hearings in which the testimony is kept secret, at least until the hearing is concluded and sometimes longer. In addition, the person who may be accused of crime and is the subject of the hearing is denied his constitutional right to confront his accusers and cross-examine them. In states in which prosecutors may proceed through either the grand jury or a preliminary examination (and the filing of an *information* as the accusatory pleading), the grand jury indictment is often selected as the route of accusation because the prosecutor can build up a case against the accused without subjecting the state's witnesses to identification, confrontation, and cross-examination.

When a grand jury is stacked with friends of judges, the sheriff, and others in law enforcement, and its members are financially well off, there is quite a "law and order" and antiblack quotient which favors the prosecutor seeking an indictment against a black person accused of crime in a case without sufficient evidence. A prosecutor tells these elite jurors that the state need only present evidence sufficient to convince them the suspect *may* be guilty, and the trial court will do the rest.

Recommendation: The method of selecting grand jurors must be free of bias in favor of any group in the community, and it must produce a jury that is a fair cross section of a community, *not* merely a sampling of a fair cross section. Furthermore, the prosecutors should not circumvent fundamental procedural safeguards in states which permit prosecutors to proceed by preliminary examination and information in lieu of the grand jury indictment and to bring a case before a grand jury without publicly stating reasons for the use of the grand jury.

TRIAL JURIES AND MINORITY DEFENDANTS

Although the right to be tried by a jury of one's peers is deeply embedded in Anglo-American law, disadvantaged minorities are still excluded from juries throughout the United States in cases in which the defendant is black or brown. In *Ex parte Virginia*,[14] a Virginia county court judge, charged by the law of that state with the selection of jurors to serve for the year 1878 in the circuit and county courts of his county, was indicted in the district court for excluding and failing to select as jurors certain citizens of his county of African race and black color.

[14]100 (Otto) U.S. 339 (1879).

These blacks possessed all other qualifications prescribed by law but were excluded from the jury lists on account of their race, color, and previous conditions of servitude.

The United States Supreme Court refused to grant the judge in this case legal relief under a writ of *habeas corpus* as he was not acting judicially but performing a ministerial act in selecting the jury list, and he was bound to obey the federal Constitution's Fourteenth Amendment in the discharge of that duty and the laws passed in pursuance thereof. This constitutional amendment, the court noted, was ordained to secure equal rights to all persons and, to ensure to all persons the enjoyment of such rights, power was given to Congress to enforce its provisions by appropriate legislation.

In the dissenting opinion in this case, Justice Field, with whom Justice Clifford concurred, makes an interesting comment about the "notion" that when a colored person is accused of a criminal offense, the presence of persons of his race on the jury by which he is to be tried is essential to secure to him the equal protection of the laws:

> The position that in cases where the rights of colored persons are concerned, justice will not be done to them unless they have a mixed jury, is founded upon the notion that in such cases white persons will not be fair and honest jurors. If this position be correct, there ought not to be any white persons on the jury where the interest of colored persons only are involved. That jury would not be an honest or fair one, of which any of its members should be governed in his judgment by other considerations than the law and the evidence; and that decision would hardly be considered just which should be reached by a sort of compromise, in which the prejudice of one race were set off against the prejudice of the other. To be consistent, those who hold this notion should contend that in cases affecting members of the colored race only, the juries should be composed entirely of colored persons, and that the presiding judge should be of the same race. To this result the doctrine asserted by the District Court (in the majority opinion) logically leads.[15]

Systematic exclusion of blacks from a trial jury would result in any jury verdict having a good cause for reversal upon appeal: the conviction would be invalid under the due process and equal protection clauses of the Fourteenth Amendment. In *Peters* v. *Kiff*,[16] the United States Supreme Court upheld this doctrine although the accused in this case was not a black, but a white defendant. In this case the majority opinion comments:

[15]*Ex parte Virginia*, p. 369.
[16]407 U.S., 493 (1972).

This court has never before considered a white defendant's challenge to the exclusion of Negroes from jury service. The essence of petitioner's claim is this: that the tribunals which indicted and convicted him were constituted in a manner that is prohibited by the Constitution and by statute; that the impact of that error on any individual trial is unascertainable; and that consequently any indictment or conviction returned by such tribunals must be set aside.

The use of peremptory challenges by a prosecutor to exclude blacks or browns from a trial jury in which a minority person is the defendant has become popular, but is self-limiting since the prosecutor has only a fixed number of such challenges (the number depends on the law of the local jurisdiction), and—as any trial attorney—a prosecutor hoards these challenges. There is no doubt, however, that many all-white juries result from the use of peremptory challenges by a prosecutor.

To some extent, the prosecution's *voir dire* examination cannot do a great deal more than attempt to show that prospective minority jurors are biased or prejudiced in favor of the defendant or are against the legal system itself or some portion of it. However, skilled questioners obtain unusual results and can have the judge dismiss many prospective minority jurors from a trial jury as a result of showing bias and prejudice on *voir dire*—a challenge for cause.

In opposition, the defense attorney has an equal number of peremptory challenges (except in cases involving multiple defendants, the "defense" allocation of such challenges is usually divided equally among the defendants) and a better opportunity to show bias and prejudice by white prospective jurors against black and brown defendants on *voir dire* examination. In this questioning, a skilled defense attorney can develop grounds to request the presiding judge to dismiss the prospective juror for cause. The defense attorney can probe not only for actual or direct bias or prejudice, but also for hidden or indirect bias and prejudice by questioning whether the juror has any black or brown friends, has ever visited the home of a black or brown person, been visited in his own home by a black or brown family, had dinner with a black or brown, invited a black or brown friend to his home for dinner, etc.

Recommendation: Government should not subject a minority defendant to trial by a jury selected in an arbitrary and discriminatory manner which violates the Constitution and laws of the United States, because illegal and unconstitutional jury selection procedures cast doubt on the integrity of the judicial process. Further, blacks and browns should be included on a trial jury not only when the issues involve race or ethnic background, but also when the issues are more general, for they bring to the courtroom a perspective on human events unique to minority jurors.

RELEASE OF MINORITY ARRESTEES ON BAIL

One of the obvious problems in criminal justice has been the failure to release on bail poor persons arrested and accused of crime. Hundreds of persons remain in jail until trial because they do not have the funds or property to post as bail to secure their pretrial release. Professional bail bondsmen profit from "cash" bail procedures almost as the Shylocks (money lenders) of organized crime. Arrestees without sufficient funds to post their own bail pay a fee (at least the legal maximum, and often additional high under-the-table charges) to "borrow" a bail bond in a sum equal to their bail. Since minorities are mainly poor persons, this profit-making adjunct of the judicial function of setting bail denies them equal justice—the right to pretrial release with all of its advantages in helping defense counsel prepare for trial and none of the disadvantages of life in jail.

Northern civil rights workers accused of crimes in southern states were kept in jail because of bail injustices and brutally attacked by jailers or other prisoners encouraged by jailers. In 1962 and 1963, cash bail for arrestees in the freedom ride cases in the South was close to a million dollars.

To pile injustice on the basic inequity of posting cash bail, the minority poor are often victimized by:

1. Having to post the legal maximum bail set in bail schedules
2. Being held in exorbitant bail, such as fifty- or a hundred-thousand dollars, when conspiracy to commit murder and other major crimes are alleged (Several defendants in the New York Black Panther case were held for almost two years because of this high bail procedure.)
3. Being held on a felony charge at the time of arrest and forced to pay a larger amount of cash bail, although the felony charge will be reduced to a misdemeanor charge when processed by the court or prosecutor
4. Being held on multiple charges (loitering, disorderly conduct, assault on a peace officer, inciting to riot) and increasing the bail by adding the legal maximum on each charge to determine the bail sufficient for release.

Recommendation: Bail before trial should be recognized as a right for all minority defendants whenever the laws specify a case is bailable, despite claims that such defendants will not appear in court for trial. Pretrial cash bail for minority defendants should be stopped as a judicial practice, and such defendants should be released on their own recognizance.

FAIR TRIAL

If a person accused of crime accepts the American judicial concept of a neutral trial judge and the adversary system of trial procedure as a valid and reliable means of determining truth on the issue of guilt or innocence, he will stand trial rather than flee or otherwise subvert that legal process, and he will accept the penalties accessed in a spirit likely to further his rehabilitation. On the other hand, if a person accused of crime does not view the trial judge as neutral, nor the prosecutor as an ethical adversary of the defense, he may attempt to publicize his plight and make the jury aware of it, or he may seek legal remedies on the claim of a political trial.

While the rules for guiding judicial action and restraint in the conduct of criminal trials require the trial judge to adhere to the cannons and codes applicable to this role[17] and to his membership in the state bar, the "hanging" judge can often satisfy the requirements in the record of the trial while at the same time presiding over an unfair trial. Appellate review is often handicapped in reversing a political trial when it appears on the transcript of the record that the trial judge has been technically correct in his rulings and supervision.

Similarly, standards for the role of prosecutor state it is unprofessional for a prosecutor to use illegal means to obtain evidence or to employ, instruct, or encourage others to use such means.[18] Yet, in the 1973 exposure of the operations of federal super-secret police, prosecutors of ghetto militants and alleged radicals, such as the Chicago Seven (which included Black Panther leader Bobby Seale), were ready to accept the rewards of breaking and entering by federal employees to secure evidence which would bulwark the prosecution's case or destroy the defense. A prosecutor's use of accomplice witnesses, infiltrating

[17] *See* Advisory Committee on the Judge's Function, *Standards Relating to the Function of the Trial Judge—Tentative Draft* (New York: American Bar Association, 1972).

[18] Advisory Committee on the Prosecution and Defense Functions, *Standards Relating to the Prosecution Function and the Defense Function* (New York: American Bar Association, 1971), p. 30.

spies, and undercover police agents is often precariously balanced between legal and illegal means of obtaining evidence.

Further, delay in trials of ghetto and *barrio* militants and presenting evidence to a grand jury (when the route of preliminary examination and the filing of an information offers the black or brown defendant a more democratic process) offer the appearance of legality, but are certainly not exemplary of the conduct expected of an ethical prosecutor.

Recommendation: Whenever a defendant of a disadvantaged minority group and his legal counsel file a claim with the governor of a state that a planned trial will be a political trial and make an affirmative showing based mainly on the defendant's racial background which makes him unlikely to receive a fair trial, the public executive should be empowered to substitute special counsel in the place of the local prosecutor if he finds that such action is required to protect the public interest in upholding constitutional guarantees to a fair trial. This recommendation would not prevent motions by the defense for standard legal remedies relating to the assigned trial judge's ability to preside impartially in a criminal case. Nor would it prevent motions by the defense when the pretrial situation indicates many members of the community have become biased toward the defendant and that it will be difficult or impossible to draw a jury likely to further a fair trial.

DISCUSSION QUESTIONS

1. What is the rationale for the United States Supreme Court's decision in which parolees were granted the right to due process in parole hearings?
2. Justify the recommended standards for police use of firearms; for police field interrogations; for prevention of physical mistreatment of suspects and prisoners.
3. What are the recommended standards for selecting juries?
4. Is police surveillance of political activities justified? Explain.
5. Discuss the advantages and disadvantages of replacing a prosecutor allegedly prejudiced against minority defendants.

CASE REFERENCES

Adams v. *Williams,* 407 U.S. 143 (1972).

Cleveland v. *Miami (City of) Florida,* 263 So. 2d 573 (1972).

Ex parte Virginia, 100 (Otto) U.S. 339 (1879).

Laird v. *Tatum*, 408 U.S. 1 (1972).
Morrissey v. *Brewer*, 408 U.S. 471 (1972).
Peters v. *Kiff*, 407 U.S. 493 (1972).
Terry v. *Ohio*, 392 U.S. 1 (1968).

8

New Perspectives for Criminal Justice and Minorities

MINORITY REPRESENTATION IN CRIMINAL JUSTICE AGENCIES
POLICE-GHETTO RELATIONS
COMMUNITY RESPONSIBILITY IN INTERGROUP CONFLICTS
FREE SPEECH AND A FREE PRESS
EQUAL JUSTICE UNDER LAW

Representativeness, responsiveness, and acceptance of responsibility are the keys to new perspectives in the interrelationships among agents of criminal justice and minority groups. *Representativeness* entails the hiring and promoting of more black and brown people by criminal justice agencies to demonstrate the sincerity of the local government in guaranteeing equal treatment under law for blacks and browns. *Responsiveness* to the need of blacks and browns means that new perspectives in neighborhood government will be welcomed and that the future behavior of police in ghettos and *barrios* will be a "service" style of policing in response to accepting neighborhood residents as members of an advisory or control board. The *acceptance of responsibility* by a community and its leaders to prevent and reduce intergroup conflicts offers new horizons for prompt and decisive action when tensions build up in relations between minority groups and the dominant white population.

MINORITY REPRESENTATION IN CRIMINAL JUSTICE AGENCIES

Affirmative action programs to recruit minorities for employment are greatly needed in all criminal justice agencies, particularly in police departments, prisons, and parole and probation units. In 1972, the U.S. Department of Health, Education, and Welfare prepared an executive order setting guidelines for college and university affirmative action programs to ensure improved minority (women and ethnic minorities: black, Asian-American, Mexican American, and Native American) representation among the white Ph.D.'s on the nation's campuses. The concept implied that a benign neutrality in selecting new faculty members would not qualify the school as an equal opportunity employer, and federal funds would be cut off until affirmative action was taken to hire minority faculty. "Benign neutrality" meant the old creed, "We select only the very best men from the available applicants," an academic euphemism for friends, friends of friends, and former students.

In applying this concept to criminal justice agency hiring, affirmative action requires more than ensuring employment *neutrality* with regard to color, race, religion, sex, and national origin; it requires that police, prison, probation, and parole agencies make *additional* efforts to *recruit, employ,* and *promote* qualified members of groups formerly excluded, even if such exclusion cannot be traced to particular discriminatory practices on the part of a particular hiring agency. The concept behind affirmative action in hiring minorities is that, unless such action is undertaken to overcome the effects of past systematic institutional forms of exclusion and discrimination, a benign neutrality in employment practices will perpetuate the status quo ante indefinitely.[1]

To implement an affirmative action program, the hiring agency needs little more than the determination to rectify the past underutilization of women and ethnic minorities and:

1. An inventory of current personnel and an evaluation of the present situation
2. A list of goals stated in percentages of minority representation to the full capacity of the hiring agency and in percentages of various promotional ranks
3. A good-faith implementation program.

An inventory of all personnel would report the following:

---

[1]Higher Education Guidelines, Executive Order No. 11246, Department of Health, Education, and Welfare, 1 October 1972, p. 3.

1. Identifiable patterns of job classification by sex or ethnic minority status of current employees
2. Under-utilization of women or ethnic minorities
3. Patterns of differences among current white (majority group) employees and current women or ethnic minority employees listing rank; type of promotional "ladder" available; salary levels; rate of advancement; termination conditions (exit interviews); rights and privileges.

An evaluation of the above inventory would compare the current employee distribution throughout the organization (white, female, and minority employees) with the estimated percentage of women and minority persons that would class the hiring agency as an equal employment organization. In this comparison, the current employee data should be compared with the availability of noncollege women and minority applicants in the local labor market and among community-college and four-year-college and university graduates in police science or criminal justice.

In the *National Association for the Advancement of Colored People (NAACP)* v. *Allen,*[2] a United States District Court took action on a claim of racial discrimination in the hiring of Alabama state police personnel. The court held that racial discrimination did exist and said that mandatory and prohibitory injunctive relief would be granted to restrain discriminatory practices and to require a stated *percentage* (25%) of black troopers to be hired.

In this case the court commented on past practices in hiring troopers:

> Plaintiffs have shown without contradiction that the defendants have engaged in a blatant and continuous pattern and practice of discrimination in hiring in the Alabama Department of Public Safety, both as to troopers and supporting personnel. In the thirty-seven-year history of the patrol there has never been a black trooper and the only Negroes ever employed by the department have been nonmerit system laborers. This unexplained and unexplainable discriminatory conduct by state officials is unquestionably a violation of the Fourteenth Amendment.

The order of judgment and decree of the court in *NAACP* v. *Allen* was:

1. That defendants' motion to dismiss be and the same is hereby denied.
2. That the defendants John S. Frazer, as Director, Alabama Personnel Department and Walter L. Allen, as Director, Alabama Department of Public Safety, their agents, officers, successors in office, employees

[2]340 F. Supp. 703 (1972).

and all persons acting in concert or participation with them, be and they are hereby enjoined from engaging in any employment practices, including recruitment, examination, appointment, training, promotion, retention or any other personnel action, for the purpose or with the effect of discriminating against any employee, or actual or potential applicant for employment, on the ground of race or color.

3. It is further ordered that the defendants be and they are each hereby enjoined from failing to hire and permanently employ after the probationary period, one Negro trooper for each white trooper hired until approximately twenty-five (25) percent of the Alabama state trooper force is comprised of Negroes. This injunction applies to the cadet and auxiliary troopers as well as to the regular troopers. It shall be the responsibility of the Department of Public Safety and Personnel Department to find and hire the necessary qualified black troopers.

4. It is further ordered that the defendants be and they are hereby enjoined from conducting any training courses for the purpose of training new troopers until the groups to be given said training courses are comprised of approximately twenty-five (25) percent black trooper candidates.

5. It is further ordered that the defendants be and they are each hereby permanently enjoined from failing to hire supporting personnel for the Department of Public Safety in the ratio of one Negro for each white until approximately twenty-five (25) percent of the supporting personnel are black. The decree in *United States* v. *Frazer*, 317 F. Supp. 1079 . . . is hereby amended insofar as the Department of Public Safety's employment practices are concerned.

6. It is further ordered that eligible and promotional registers heretofore used for the purpose of hiring troopers be and they are hereby abrogated to the extent necessary to comply with this decree.

7. It is further ordered that:
   a. The defendants shall assign employees on the base of their training and ability, without regard to race. Negro employees shall not be assigned to serve exclusively or predominately Negro clientele.
   b. The defendants shall advise the public in all advertisements and announcements that they will appoint and employ persons on an equal opportunity merit basis, without discrimination on the ground of race or color. In such public announcements, the defendants shall advise potential and actual applicants and employees of their right to be free from discrimination. Said announcements shall be made throughout the State of Alabama within thirty days from the date of this order.
   c. The defendants shall adopt and implement a program of recruitment and advertising which will fully advise the Negro citizens of the State of Alabama of the employment opportunities now available to them with the Alabama Department of Public Safety. The defendants shall institute regular recruitment visits to predomi-

nantly Negro schools (vocational, high and college) throughout the State of Alabama, such visits to be made in person by appropriate officials of the Alabama Department of Public Safety.

d. No commitments of employment given by either of the defendants or any of their agents to any applicant or potential applicant, short of actual hiring prior to January 13, 1972, the date the temporary restraining order was entered in the state trooper case, shall be given any priority over the hiring ratio set out in this decree. The present hiring lists, compiled as a result of the discriminatory practices, may be used to hire the white troopers, white trooper cadets and white supporting personnel. New lists, however, must be compiled and utilized for the black troopers, black trooper cadets and black supporting personnel.

e. The defendants shall file through their counsel with this Court within ninety days from the date of this decree a written report setting forth in detail the efforts which have been undertaken to recruit and hire black applicants. The report shall also include the number of vacancies filled among the state troopers, the auxiliary troopers, the cadets and the supporting personnel of the Department of Public Safety during this period and the number of each race hired into each of these groups.

f. It is further ordered that the costs of this proceeding be and they are hereby taxed to the defendants in Civil Action No. 3561–N, for which execution may issue.

The Court retains jurisdiction over these cases.[3]

At the present time, several law suits are pending in other parts of the country similar to *NAACP* v. *Allen* in which women or members of ethnic minorities are plaintiffs, and the heads of police agencies, prisons, and correctional authorities are defendants. Most likely, depending on the past practices of these agencies and the current percentages of women and minorities employed and promoted, the courts will follow the lead of the United States District Court in Alabama and establish a percentage goal of equal employment and also supervise the case to ensure that the court order is not sabotaged.

A good-faith implementation of an affirmative action hiring program geared to rapidly increase the number of women and ethnic minorities hired and promoted by an agency of criminal justice should—

1. define *qualified applicant* in terms of normal standards of the hiring agency but refrain from writing job specifications more narrow than warranted by the needs of the hiring agency and should not continue

[3] *NAACP* v. *Allen*, p. 707.

or initiate applicant standards likely to exclude women or ethnic minorities (In New York City, the minimum height limit was a bar to most Puerto Rican applicants for many years.);
2. make an honest, good-faith effort to locate qualified persons by—
   a. advertising in local papers and law enforcement journals;
   b. contacting two- and four-year colleges with criminal justice programs for applicants among their graduates;
   c. contacting relevant professional organizations and their leaders (law, nursing, and teaching) as bird dogs who will deliver recruiting data to women and ethnic minority students in these fields or to associates now employed at lower salary levels than those of the criminal justice agency;
   d. actively soliciting job applicants in all neighborhood organizations of women and minorities, all local high schools, and all mass employers (U.S.A.F. bases, factories, etc.);
   e. making an explicit commitment to equal employment opportunity in all recruiting announcements and advertisements by including the phrase *equal opportunity employer*;
   f. notifying all prospective applicants that discrimination in the hiring agency, whether purposeful or inadvertent, has been eliminated and directing all operations personnel, supervisors, and middle-managers of the agency to abide by this policy of nondiscrimination.

Recommendation: All criminal justice agencies, particularly police departments, prisons, and probation and parole agencies should immediately implement an affirmative action program to hire women and ethnic minorities up to an appropriate percentage level in order to increase the promotional opportunities for these minorities and to close the gap between existing differences in working conditions between white employees and these minorities. Further, failure to achieve acceptable standards as an equal opportunity employer without delay would warrant action by a local organization of the disadvantaged minorities to secure a court order directing the agency to stop discrimination in employment.

POLICE-GHETTO RELATIONS

Why must a black ghetto or brown *barrio* be patrolled by a centralized white-dominated police force in order to protect the black or brown resident population? If the answer is not *containment* or *control* of the minority, then it can only be that the ghetto or *barrio* as a neighborhood is too weak politically to resist this domination effectively. Black African nations which have replaced white colonial governments with those of their own people are policed by black persons. Why not ghettos?

An eminent authority on police organization and management states that "institutional" policing (as opposed to "communal" or "neighborhood policing") is vital, because:

> The law must be vigorously enforced because to do otherwise would call into question the law itself. Though community and familial norms are the ultimate foundation of public order, the fact of high and rising crime rates shows that such norms are less and less able to serve the functions they once performed in a more stable and traditional social system.[4]

Within this concept of institutional policing is an authoritative approval for a "get-tough" police policy in ghetto or *barrio*:

> Indeed, the law must be enforced with special vigor in those areas where community norms appear weakest; failure to do so would penalize law-abiding persons in those areas and inhibit the development of a regard for community norms among the law breakers.[5]

It is little wonder that a black author wrote about the white policeman:

> He moves through Harlem, therefore, like an occupying soldier in a bitterly hostile country; which is precisely what, and where, he is, and the reason he walks in twos and threes. And he is not the only one who knows why he is always in company: the people who are watching him know why, too. Any street meeting sacred or secular, which he and his colleagues uneasily cover has as its explicit or implicit burden the cruelty and injustice of the white domination. The white policeman standing on a Harlem street corner finds himself at the very center of the revolution now occurring in the world. He is not prepared for it.[6]

[4]James Q. Wilson, *Varieties of Police Behavior: The Management of Law and Order in Eight Communities* (Cambridge, Mass.: Harvard University Press, 1968), p. 285.

[5]Wilson, *Police Behavior*, pp. 285–86.

[6]Baldwin, *Nobody Knows My Name*, pp. 66–67.

For years, applicants likely to speak out about unfair working conditions or who might otherwise disturb the status quo have been rejected.[7] The police "rebellion," in which police struck out for union membership, is more than half a century behind the trade union movement in the United States. For an even longer term, working policemen have been silenced by their superiors and department regulations stating they are not to discuss "politics," or by the threat of dismissal inherent in Oliver Wendell Holmes's statement that there is a "constitutional right to talk politics, but no constitutional right to be a policeman."[8]

The silence of police working in ghettos has led to local government denial of the need to restructure policing of these areas. The only vocal demands are now of groups such as the Black Panthers, and against police silence and resistance, the cry for help to re-police the black residential areas has gone unheeded.

As presently structured, police-ghetto relations represent two racially based systems that are mutually incompatible because of a basic contradiction in their social goals and status orientations. The white system wants to maintain the subservient status of blacks; the black system wants fuller social participation and a restructured role and status for blacks. When police control is totally within the white system, blacks are disadvantaged because police control standards are linked to the goal of the white system. Black citizens do not, therefore, have equal protection or justice.[9]

So-called sensitivity or human relations training or extensive programs in police-community relations do not change the facts of policing in ghettos nor the control and containment function of policing under a white-dominated goal system. Most ghetto residents are not seeking to rid their residential areas of police, but are asking that bad police practices be eliminated, that avenues of complaint be opened and the range of police discretionary authority contained, and that the tensions generated in the ghettos not be aggravated by over-zealous policing and official violence. Unless there is a restructuring of policing in ghetto areas akin to Sir Robert Peel's revolution in police work in London in 1829, cities will never be free from the apprehension of racial violence.

[7]*Anthony* v. *Bouza*, "The Policeman's Character Investigation: Lowered Standards or Changing Times," *The Journal of Criminal Law, Criminology, and Police Science*, Vol. 63, No. 1 (1972), pp. 120–24; and in the same issue, Robert W. Balch, "The Police Personality: Fact or Fiction," p. 115.

[8]As Justice of the Massachusetts Supreme Court, in *McAuliff* v. *City of New Bedford*, 155 Mass. 216, 29 N.E.517 (1892).

[9]Robert Mast, "Police-Ghetto Relations: Some Findings and a Proposal for Structural Change," *Race*, Vol. 11, No. 4 (1970), p. 447.

The narrow institutional definition of effective policing must be broadened considerably if future racial violence is to be avoided.[10]
An authoritative text in police management writes of the police image:

> The effectiveness of a law enforcement agency is determined by the public cooperation and support it receives. If a department cannot gain and maintain the confidence of the citizens in its community, its effectiveness is curtailed and its integrity and ability questioned.
>
> Public trust and support can be obtained when the citizens are confident that the police will not overstep the safeguards to individual liberty and when the individual members of a department demonstrate that they are interested in and actively engaged in promoting the public peace and welfare.[11]

About a quarter of a century ago, New York City police referred to the interactions between members of the police department and members of the community as "public relations." Public relations was defined as "the sum total of the attitudes, impressions, and opinions of the public and its relationship with the department."[12]
In this 1949 guide for police, it was pointed out that police officers on duty in an area predominantly inhabited by any racial or religious group were cautioned to display the department policy of uniformity and equality in the enforcement of the law and were asked to show sympathetic interest in and to give prompt attention to the daily problems of "the people." They were also told to make every effort to dissipate any impression of indifference or neglect in dealing with complaints of people in their area of patrol and were advised to avoid any reference to race, creed, or nationality in their daily business.
Commanding officers of areas inhabited by different racial groups were advised to cultivate the friendship of outstanding citizens, businessmen, and church, civic, and group leaders. Officers were to ascertain conditions, tensions, and adequacy of police service and also to cultivate friendships which could be extremely helpful to the police in case of public disorder. The theme of these instructions was that the department had a policy of impartiality which would be strictly followed. This policy demonstrates that twenty-five years ago police offi-

[10]Paul Jacobs, "The Los Angeles Police," *The Atlantic Monthly,* December 1966, Vol. 218, pp. 95–101.

[11]George W. O'Connor and Charles G. Vanderbosch, *The Patrol Operation* (Washington, D.C.: International Association of Chiefs of Police, 1967), p. 10.

[12]*The Manual of Procedure* (New York: New York City Police Department, 1949), p. 311.

cials in a major city were aware of the special cultural forms which might dominate areas housing minority groups and that such cultural particularities were especially significant to the police responsible for these areas.

The major goal of what are now called "police-community relations" is to reduce tensions between ghetto residents and police officers. Unfortunately, police-community relation programs, with their emphasis upon in-service training and upgrading (professionalism), have failed to achieve this objective. In fact, there is a strong need for a new conceptual framework about the interactions between police and those members of the community who are at odds with the police. It must be acknowledged that any relationship between the police and ghetto residents is a power relationship because of police ability to initiate action even when no complaint is involved.

This new conceptual framework should have three major areas: (1) police style, (2) representativeness, and (3) responsiveness. *Style* involves developing a police force that would be responsive to local needs. The police would develop a service rather than the legalistic style common to the institutional mode of policing ghettos. *Responsiveness* means that the police would service the needs and demands of the ghetto community and view the black or brown population as people to serve, not to control or to contain. *Representativeness* means that the black or brown minority groups would be well represented on the police force and have direct access to the power positions within the police department.[13]

A committee of the American Bar Association studying the urban police function has recommended nationwide standards for police behavior and sanctions to enforce control of police activity:

> *Need for accountability.* Since a principal function of police is the safe-guarding of democratic processes, if police fail to conform their conduct to the requirements of law, they subvert the democratic process and frustrate the achievement of a principal police function. It is for this reason that high priority must be given for ensuring that the police are made fully accountable to their police administrator and to the public for their actions.
>
> *Sanctions.* It should be recognized that no existing single sanction or combination of sanctions is likely to ensure completely satisfactory review

[13]Rita Mae Kelly, *Police Community Relations: Findings From the Conduct and Evaluation of an OEO-Funded Experiment in Washington, D.C.* (Kensington, Md.: American Institute for Research, 1972) pp. 4–6.

and control over police activities. The sanctions now existing include: (i) the exclusion of evidence obtained by unconstitutional means; (ii) criminal and tort liability for knowingly engaging in unlawful conduct; (iii) injunctive actions to terminate a pattern of unlawful conduct; and (iv) local procedures for handling complaints against police officers, procedures which usually operate administratively within police departments.[14]

Recommendation: Police in urban areas should be restructured into neighborhood units, each with its own top executive. A policy or advisory committee should be selected by a voting process open only to local residents. A good-faith, affirmative-action hiring policy should actively seek to recruit police from among local minority residents. A conceptual framework should be developed to include a service style of policing, responsiveness to ghetto residents, and a representative police force throughout its ranks; accountability for police behavior to police superiors and the people served by police in the ghetto is an important aspect of this new philosophy.

COMMUNITY RESPONSIBILITY IN INTERGROUP CONFLICTS

People from government, business, law, education, and religion are needed to work as interventionists in the field of intergroup relations. A committee of such people intent on improving both local and national intergroup relations can effectively use the media to help the public understand problems of prejudice and discrimination and how to reduce or eliminate them.

Recommendation: An intergroup committee should be organized locally to provide leadership and direction in seeking court decisions and legislation which bar discrimination; in planning and waging campaigns to educate the public about the provisions of the Fair Housing Law, Fair Employment Practices, and other civil rights legislation; and in bringing together representatives of all groups in conflict to discuss problems and to negotiate solutions.

The problem of recruiting a qualified staff for an intergroup program is serious. Although the positions are voluntary and unpaid, members must have many skills as well as sensitivity to social and human prob-

[14]American Bar Association Committee on the Police Function, *Standards Relating to the Urban Police Function, Tentative Draft* (New York: American Bar Association, 1972), pp. 15–17. *See also* Bernard Cohen, "The Police Internal System of Justice in New York City," *Journal of Criminal Law, Criminology and Police Science,* Vol. 63, No. 1, pp. 54–67.

lems. The rewards of such work, however, should make it attractive to concerned citizens.

FREE SPEECH AND A FREE PRESS

In the 1964 case of *New York Times* v. *Sullivan*,[15] the United States Supreme Court ruled that under the First Amendment *and* the Fourteenth Amendment a state cannot award damages to a public official for defamatory falsehood (libel) relating to his official conduct unless he proves the statement was made with "actual malice"—that is, with knowledge that the statement was false or with reckless disregard of whether it was false or not.

The respondent in this case was L. B. Sullivan, one of three commissioners in Montgomery, Alabama. He brought suit in a state court, as the city commissioner responsible for the supervision of the Montgomery Police Department, and alleged that he had been libeled by an advertisement in the corporate petitioner's newspaper, the *New York Times*, in text which appeared over the names of the four individual petitioners and many others. (See figure 3.) The advertisement included some false statements about police action allegedly directed against students who participated in a civil rights demonstration and against a leader of the civil rights movement. Respondent claimed the statements referred to him because his duties included supervision of the police department. The trial judge instructed the jury that such statements were "libelous per se," legal injury implied without proof of actual damages, and that for the purpose of compensatory damages malice was presumed, so that such damages could be awarded against petitioners if the statements were found to have been published by them and to have related to respondent. The judge instructed that mere negligence was not evidence of actual malice and would not justify an award of punitive damages; he refused to instruct that actual intent to harm or recklessness had to be found before punitive damages could be awarded, or that a verdict for respondent should differentiate between compensatory and punitive damages. The jury awarded respondent damages of $500,000, the full amount claimed. The Alabama Supreme Court affirmed this decision.

In reversing the decisions of the state courts, the Court not only upheld the right of freedom of speech of all citizens under the First Amendment but also blocked an apparent attempt to prevent national publications from writing about the plight of America's blacks, the fight

[15]376 U.S. 254 (1964).

for equality, and the struggle against the injustice of harassing arrests and political trials for black protest leaders. The majority opinion pointed out the national commitment to the principle that debate on public issues should be robust, uninhibited, and wide open, and "it may well include vehement, caustic, and sometimes unpleasantly sharp attacks on government and public officials."

The Court quoted an extract from a prior case to illustrate profound commitment:

> Those who won our independence believed that public discussion is a political duty; and that this should be a fundamental principle of the American government. They recognized the risks to which all human institutions are subject. But they knew that order cannot be secured merely through fear of punishment for its infraction; that it is hazardous to discourage thought, hope and imagination; that fear breeds repression; that repression breeds hate; that hate menaces stable government; that the path of safety lies in the opportunity to discuss freely supposed grievances and proposed remedies; and that the fitting remedy for evil counsels is good ones. Believing in the power of reason as applied through public discussion, they eschewed silence coerced by law—the argument of force in its worst form. Recognizing the occasional tyrannies of governing majorities, they amended the Constitution so that free speech and assembly should be guaranteed.[16]

Another case which might also have served to silence the national press about injustice to blacks by official violence of police was *Time, Inc., v. Pape*.[17] The decision in this case illustrates the willingness of the United States Supreme Court to support the right to publish critical appraisals of government agents in extension of First and Fourteenth Amendment guarantees.

In a discussion of "police brutality and related violence" in its 1961 report, the Civil Rights Commission mentioned the case of *Monroe v. Pape* and listed some of the allegations of Monroe's civil rights complaint filed against certain Chicago policemen headed by Deputy Chief of Detectives Pape. In an article about the report, *Time* magazine quoted from a summary of the complaint without indicating that the charges were Monroe's and not the independent findings of the commission. Pape sued *Time* for libel.

---

[16] *Whitney* v. *California*, 274 U.S. 357 (1927), pp. 375–76.
[17] 401 U.S. 279 (1971).

Heed Their Rising Voices

"The growing movement of peaceful mass demonstrations by Negroes is something new in the South, something understandable.... Let Congress heed their rising voices, for they will be heard."

—New York Times editorial
Saturday, March 19, 1960

As the whole world knows by now, thousands of Southern Negro students are engaged in widespread non-violent demonstrations in positive affirmation of the right to live in human dignity as guaranteed by the U.S. Constitution and the Bill of Rights. In their efforts to uphold these guarantees, they are being met by an unprecedented wave of terror by those who would deny and negate that document which the whole world looks upon as setting the pattern for modern freedom....

In Orangeburg, South Carolina, when 400 students peacefully sought to buy doughnuts and coffee at lunch counters in the business district, they were forcibly ejected, tear-gassed, soaked to the skin in freezing weather with fire hoses, arrested en masse and herded into an open barbed-wire stockade for hours in the bitter cold.

In Montgomery, Alabama, after students sang "My Country, 'Tis of Thee" on the State Capitol steps, their leaders were expelled from school, and truckloads of police armed with shotguns and tear-gas ringed the Alabama State College Campus. When the entire student body protested to state authorities by refusing to re-register, their dining hall was padlocked in an attempt to starve them into submission.

In Tallahassee, Atlanta, Nashville, Savannah, Greensboro, Memphis, Richmond, Charlotte, and a host of other cities in the South, young American teenagers, in face of the entire weight of official state apparatus and police power, have boldly stepped forth as protagonists of democracy. Their courage and amazing restraint have inspired millions and given a new dignity to the cause of freedom.

Small wonder that the Southern violators of the Constitution fear this new, non-violent brand of

Figure 3. This advertisement appeared in the *New York Times* on March 29, 1960 and was used by a southern public official as grounds for a lawsuit, *New York Times* v. *Sullivan*. The remainder of the advertisement lists the names of sponsors and a coupon to accompany

150

freedom fighter…even as they fear the upswelling right-to-vote movement. Small wonder that they are determined to destroy the one man who, more than any other, symbolizes the new spirit now sweeping the South—the Rev. Dr. Martin Luther King, Jr., world-famous leader of the Montgomery Bus Protest. For it is his doctrine of non-violence which has inspired and guided the students in their widening wave of sit-ins; and it is this same Dr. King who founded and is president of the Southern Christian Leadership Conference—the organization which is spearheading the surging right-to-vote movement. Under Dr. King's direction the Leadership Conference conducts Student Workshops and Seminars in the philosophy and technique of non-violent resistance.

Again and again the Southern violators have answered Dr. King's peaceful protests with intimidation and violence. They have bombed his home almost killing his wife and child. They have assaulted his person. They have arrested him seven times—for "speeding," "loitering" and similar "offenses." And now they have charged him with "perjury"—a *felony* under which they could imprison him for *ten years*. Obviously, their real purpose is to remove him physically as the leader to whom the students and millions of others—look for guidance and support, and thereby to intimidate *all* leaders who may rise in the South. Their strategy is to behead this affirmative movement, and thus to demoralize Negro Americans and weaken their will to struggle. The defense of Martin Luther King, spiritual leader of the student sit-in movement, clearly, therefore, is an integral part of the total struggle for freedom in the South.

Decent-minded Americans cannot help but applaud the creative daring of the students and the quiet heroism of Dr. King. But this is one of those moments in the stormy history of Freedom when men and women of good will must do more than applaud the rising-to-glory of others. The America whose good name hangs in the balance before a watchful world, the America whose heritage of Liberty these Southern Upholders of the Constitution are defending, is *our* America as well as theirs…

We must heed their rising voices—yes—but we must add our own.

We must extend ourselves above and beyond moral support and render the material help so urgently needed by those who are taking the risks, facing jail, and even death in a glorious re-affirmation of our Constitution and its Bill of Rights.

We urge you to join hands with our fellow Americans in the South by supporting, with your dollars, this Combined Appeal for all three needs —the defense of Martin Luther King—the support of the embattled students—and the struggle for the right-to-vote.

Your Help Is Urgently Needed
. . . . *NOW!!*

contributions to the Committee to Defend Martin Luther King and the Struggle for Freedom in the South.

At the trial, the author of the article and the researcher admitted awareness that the wording of the report had been significantly altered but insisted that its real meaning had not been changed. The district court granted *Time's* motion for a directed verdict at the close of evidence, but the court of appeals reversed, holding that the jury should determine whether the omission of the word *alleged* showed actual malice. Both courts agreed that Pape was a public official and that the article concerned his official conduct. The Court's ruling was: "In the circumstances of this case the magazine did not engage in a falsification sufficient in itself to sustain a jury finding of actual malice."

The basic guarantees of the First and Fourteenth Amendments allow criticism of public officials and exposure of wrongdoing. No public official can silence publication of such copy by threats of libel suits since the time of *New York Times Co.* v. *Sullivan* and *Time, Inc.* v. *Pape.* This was proved in 1973 when the *Washington Post* published a series of articles alleging breaking and entering and other illegal activity by former secret police agents collecting intelligence for a political party, which led to the Watergate scandal and the indictment of many public officials on the staff of the President of the United States, the United States Department of Justice, and an enforcement agency (Alcohol, Drugs, and Firearms) of the United States Treasury Department.

EQUAL JUSTICE UNDER LAW

The right to speak out against injustice and inequality and the opportunity to publish such critical comments nationally can expose the facts of racial and ethnic discrimination to public view and appraisal. No state legislator, executive, judicial officer, policeman, or prosecutor can combat the Constitution without violating his position as an agent of the criminal justice system in America nor can any law-making body annul the judgments of the courts of the United States and destroy the rights acquired under those judgments.

The United States Constitution is the supreme law of the land. State responsibility for criminal justice administration and the acts of its agents at local levels must be exercised consistently with federal constitutional requirements as they apply to state agents and actions. The Constitution created a government within the framework of a federal union that is dedicated to equal justice under law. The Fourteenth Amendment emphasizes that ideal for all citizens—particularly the country's black population. Segregation on racial grounds has been outlawed because it conflicts with the Fourteenth Amendment's command that no state shall deny to any person within its jurisdiction the equal protection of the laws; and the right of students in public education systems not to be segregated on racial grounds is now fundamental and embraced in the concept of due process of law.

Some past events, against this framework of affirmative action for equal justice, seem improbable and impossible: violence almost at random resulting in the death of rioters; police raids and shoot-outs and super-secret police surveillance; and grand jury indictments and political trials of Black Panthers and similar groups. Official violence leading to injury, imprisonment, and death resulted because blacks and browns have acted against unequal justice, against the caste system of ghetto and *barrio* living, against subordination to the dominant white majority, and against the political disenfranchisement and sharecropper's role in politics that block disadvantaged minorities from the rewards of participating in local and federal government.

The bad dream of unequal justice is America's major social problem. It has been a problem since the time of slavery, and it has persisted because of the dominant white majority's refusal to make real the freedoms guaranteed to minorities by the fundamental charter that assures the freedoms of *all* American citizens. The constitutional ideal of equal justice under law can be a living truth, but it is a national disgrace that in a time of worldwide freedom for all nations and peoples blacks and browns in America must fight and die to achieve the ideal of equal justice under law.

DISCUSSION QUESTIONS

1. What factors force greater minority representation in criminal justice agencies?
2. Why are the people of ghettos and *barrios* seeking local control of police behavior? Why are police generally opposed to such control?
3. How can community acceptance of responsibility for intergroup conflict improve minority relations with the dominant group?
4. What are the underlying reasons for protecting the rights of minorities to publicly criticize the acts of public officials?
5. How might the recommendations in Chapters 7 and 8 enhance the future realization of equal justice for minorities?

CASE REFERENCES

NAACP v. *Allen,* 340 F. Supp. 703 (1972).
New York Times Co. v. *Sullivan,* 376 U.S. 254 (1964).
Monroe v. *Pape,* 365 U.S. 167 (1961).
Time, Inc. v. *Pape,* 401 U.S. 279 (1971).

Selected References

ADAMS, RUSSELL L. *Great Negroes Past and Present* (2nd ed.). Chicago, Ill.: Afro-Am Books, 1963.

ALLPORT, GORDON W., *The Nature of Prejudice.* Reading, Mass.: Addison-Wesley Publishing Co., 1954.

AMERICAN BAR ASSOCIATION, *The Function of the Trial Judge.* New York: 1972.

AMERICAN BAR ASSOCIATION, PROJECT ON STANDARDS FOR CRIMINAL JUSTICE, *The Prosecution Function and the Defense Function.* New York: 1971.

ANDERSON, CHARLES H., *White Protestant Americans: From National Origins to Religious Group.* Englewood Cliffs, N.J.: Prentice-Hall, 1970.

APTHEKER, HERBERT, *American Negro Slave Revolts.* New York: International Publishers Co., 1967.

BALDWIN, JAMES, *The Fire Next Time.* New York: The Dial Press, 1963.

———, *Nobody Knows My Name.* New York: The Dial Press, 1961.

BECKER, THEODORE L., ed., *Political Trials.* Indianapolis, Ind.: The Bobbs-Merrill Co., 1971.

BEDAU, HUGO ADAM, ed., *Civil Disobedience: Theory and Practice.* Indianapolis, Ind.: Pegasus, 1969.

BLACKBURN, SARA, ed., *White Justice: Black Experience Today in America's Courtrooms.* New York: Harper & Row, Publishers, 1971.

BLACK CAUCUS OF THE CALIFORNIA ASSEMBLY, *Treatment of Prisoners at California Training Facility—Soledad Central.* Sacramento, Calif.: California State Legislature, 1970.

BRAWLEY, BENJAMIN, *A Social History of the American Negro.* New York: The Macmillan Co., 1921.

BREITMAN, GEORGE, ed., *By Any Means Necessary.* New York: Pathfinder Press, 1972.

BRODERICK, FRANCIS L., and AUGUST MEIER, eds., *Negro Protest Thought in the Twentieth Century.* Indianapolis, Ind.: The Bobbs-Merrill Co., 1965.

BROWN, CLAUDE, *Manchild in the Promised Land.* New York: The Macmillan Co., 1965.

CARTER, WILMOTH A., *The New Negro of the South.* Jericho, N.Y.: Exposition Press, 1967.

CHADBOURN, J. H., *Lynching and the Law.* Durham, N.C.: University of North Carolina Press, 1933.

CHAMBERS, BRADFORD, *Chronicles of Negro Protest.* New York: Parents' Magazine Press, 1968.

CHENAULT, LAWRENCE R., *The Puerto Rican Migrant in New York City.* Reprint of 1938 ed. Russell & Russell, Publishers, 1970.

CHIKOTA, RICHARD A., and MICHAEL C. MORAN, eds., *Riot in the Cities: An Analytical Symposium on the Causes and Effects.* Rutherford, N.J.: Fairleigh Dickinson University Press, 1970.

CLARK, KENNETH B., *Dark Ghetto: Dilemmas of Social Power.* New York: Harper & Row, Publishers, 1965.

CLEAVER, ELDRIDGE, *Soul on Ice.* New York: McGraw-Hill Book Co., 1967.

COHN, RAY, *A Fool for a Client: My Struggle Against the Power of a Public Prosecutor.* New York: Hawthorn Books, 1971.

COMMISSION ON CIVIL RIGHTS, *Law Enforcement: A Report on Equal Protection in the South.* Washington, D.C.: U.S. Government Printing Office, 1965.

COMMITTEE ON THE JUDICIARY, United States Senate, Eighty-Ninth Congress, Second Session, *Cuban Refugee Problems.* Washington, D.C.: U.S. Government Printing Office, 1966.

CONANT, RALPH W., *The Prospects for Revolution: A Study of Riots, Civil Disobedience and Insurrections in Contemporary America.* New York: Harper & Row, Publishers, 1971.

CONNERY, ROBERT H., *Urban Riots: Violence and Social Change.* New York: Random House, 1968

COUNTRYMAN, VERN, *Discrimination and the Law.* Chicago, Ill.: University of Chicago Press, 1965.

DALY, CHARLES U., ed., *Urban Violence.* Chicago, Ill.: University of Chicago Press, 1969.

DANIELS, ROBERT, *The Politics of Prejudice.* Berkeley, Calif.: University of California Press, 1962.

DANIELS, ROGER, and HARRY H. L. KITANO, *American Racism.* Englewood Cliffs, N.J.: Prentice-Hall, 1970.

DORSEN, NORMAN, *Discrimination and Civil Rights.* Boston, Mass.: Little, Brown & Co., 1969.

EISEMAN, ALBERTA, *From Many Lands.* New York; Atheneum Publishers, 1970.

FAGEN, R. R., RICHARD A. BRODY, and THOMAS J. O'LEARY, *Cubans in Exile: Disaffection and the Revolution.* Stanford, Calif.: Stanford University Press, 1968.

FANON, FRANTZ, *Wretched of the Earth.* Translated by Constance Farrington. New York: Grove Press, 1965.

FEIFFER, JULES, *Pictures at a Prosecution: Drawings and Text from the Chicago Conspiracy Trial.* New York: Grove Press, 1971.

FOGELSON, ROBERT M., *Violence as Protest.* Garden City, N.Y.: Doubleday & Co., 1971.

FRANKLIN, JOHN HOPE, *From Slavery to Freedom* (3rd ed.). New York: Alfred A. Knopf, 1967.

FRAZIER, FRANKLIN E., *The Negro in the United States* (rev. ed.). New York: The Macmillan Co., 1957.

FREEDMAN, MORRIS, and CAROLYN BANKS, eds., *American Mix: The Minority Experience in America.* Philadelphia, Pa.: J. B. Lippincott Co., 1972.

FRIEDMAN, LEON, *The Civil Rights Reader* (rev. ed.). New York: Walker & Co., 1968.

FROST, STANLEY, *The Challenge of the Klan.* Reprint of 1924 ed. Westport, Conn.: Greenwood Press, 1969.

FRY, HENRY P., *The Modern Ku Klux Klan.* Reprint of 1922 ed. Westport, Conn.: Greenwood Press, 1969.

GESCHWENDER, JAMES A., ed., *The Black Revolt.* Englewood Cliffs, N.J.: Prentice-Hall, 1971.

GLAZER, NATHAN, and DANIEL P. MOYNIHAN, *Beyond the Melting Pot: Puerto Ricans, Jews, Italians, and Irish of New York City.* Cambridge, Mass.: The M.I.T. Press, 1963.

GLEISSER, MARCUS, *Juries and Justice.* New York: A. S. Barnes & Co., 1968.

GLENN, NORVAL D., and CHARLES M. BONJEAN, *Blacks in the United States.* San Francisco, Calif.: Chandler Publishing Co., 1969.

GORDON, LEONARD, *A City in Racial Crisis.* Dubuque, Iowa: William C. Brown Co., Publishers, 1971.

GOVERNOR'S SELECT COMMISSION ON CIVIL DISORDER, STATE OF NEW JERSEY, *Report for Action.* Trenton, N.J.: Governor's Office, 1968.

GRANT, JOANNE, ed., *Black Protest: History, Documents and Analyses from Sixteen Nineteen to the Present.* Greenwich, Conn.: Fawcett World Library, 1968.

GRIER, WILLIAM H., and PRICE M. COBBS, *Black Rage.* New York: Basic Books, 1968.

GRIMSHAW, ALLEN D., ed., *Racial Violence in the United States.* Chicago, Ill.: Aldine-Atherton, 1969.

HANDLIN, OSCAR, *The Newcomers: Negroes and Puerto Ricans in a Changing Metropolis.* Reprint of 1959 ed. Garden City, N.Y.: Doubleday & Co., 1962.

158   American Minorities: The Justice Issue

HARING, PHILIP S., *Political Morality.* Cambridge, Mass.: Schenkman Publishing Co., 1960.

HAYS, ARTHUR GARFIELD, *Trial by Prejudice.* New York: Da Capo Press, 1970.

HEINS, MARJORIE, *Strictly Ghetto Property.* Berkeley, Calif.: Ramparts Press, 1972.

HERSEY, JOHN R., *The Algiers Motel Incident.* New York: Alfred A. Knopf, 1968.

HIGHAM, ROBIN, ed., *Bayonets in the Streets.* Lawrence, Kans.: The University Press of Kansas, 1969.

HORMACHEA, MARION C. R., *Confrontation: Violence and the Police.* Boston, Mass.: Holbrook Press, 1971.

HOROWITZ, IRVING LOUIS, *The Struggle is the Message: The Organization and Ideology of the Anti-War Movement.* Berkeley, Calif.: The Glendessary Press, 1970.

HOSOKAWA, BILL, *The Quiet Americans.* New York: William Morrow & Co., 1969.

JOHNSON, CHALMERS, *Revolutionary Change.* Boston, Mass.: Little, Brown & Co., 1966.

KEATING, EDWARD M., *Free Huey! The True Story of the Trial of Huey P. Newton for Murder.* Berkeley, Calif.: Ramparts Press, 1971.

KEMPTON, MURRAY, *The Briar Patch: The People of the State of New York v. Lumumba Shakur et al.* New York: E. P. Dutton & Co., 1973.

KENNEBECK, EDWIN, *Juror Number Four: The Trial of Thirteen Black Panthers as Seen from the Jury Box.* New York: W. W. Norton & Co., 1973.

KILLIAN, LEWIS, and CHARLES GRIGG, *Racial Crisis in America: Leadership in Conflict.* Englewood Cliffs, N.J.: Prentice-Hall, 1964.

KOTLER, MILTON, *Neighborhood Government: The Local Foundations of Political Life.* Indianapolis, Ind.: The Bobbs-Merrill Co., 1969.

KUNSTLER, WILLIAM M., *And Justice for All.* Dobbs Ferry, N.Y.: Oceana Publications, 1963.

LEITA, NATHAN, and CHARLES WOLFE, JR., *Rebellion and Authority.* Chicago, Ill.: Markham Publishing Co., 1970.

LIEBOW, ELLIOT, *Tally's Corner.* Boston, Mass.: Little, Brown & Co., 1966.

LINCOLN, C. ERIC, *The Black Muslims in America.* Boston, Mass.: Beacon Press, 1961.

LINCOLN, JAMES H., *The Anatomy of a Riot.* New York: McGraw-Hill Book Co., 1968.

LOCKE, HUBERT G., *The Detroit Riot of 1967.* Detroit, Mich.: Wayne State University Press, 1969.

McKISSICK, FLOYD, *Three-Fifths of a Man.* New York: The Macmillan Co., 1969.

MARDEN, CHARLES F., and GLADYS MEYER, *Minorities in American Society.* New York: American Book Company, 1962.

MATTHEWS, HERBERT L., *The Cuban Story.* New York: George Braziller, 1961.

MILLER, LOREN, *The Petitioners.* New York: Pantheon Books, 1966.

MILLS, CHARLES W., CLARENCE SENIOR, and ROSE K. GOLDSEN, *Puerto Rican Journey: New York's Newest Migrants.* Reprint of 1950 ed. New York: Russell & Russell, Publishers, 1967.

MOORE, GILBERT, *A Special Rage.* New York: Harper & Row, Publishers, 1971.

MOORE, JOAN W., FRANK G. MITTELBACH, and RONALD McDANIEL, *Mexican-American Study Project, Residential Segregation in the Urban Southwest.* Berkely, Calif.: University of California Press, 1966.

MYRDAL, GUNNAR, *An American Dilemma.* New York: Harper & Row, Publishers, 1944.

NELSON, JACK, and JACK BASS, *The Orangeburg Massacre.* New York: World Publishing Co., 1970.

NEWLON, CLARKE, *Famous Mexican-Americans.* New York: Dodd, Mead & Co., 1972.

NEWTON, HUEY, *Revolutionary Suicide.* New York: Harcourt Brace Jovanovich, 1973.

NOVAK, MICHAEL, *The Rise of the Unmeltable Ethnics.* New York: The Macmillan Co., 1971.

ORTH, SAMUEL P., *Our Foreigners.* New Haven, Conn.: Yale University Press, 1920.

PHILLIPS, KEVIN P., *The Emerging Republican Majority.* New Rochelle, N.Y.: Arlington House, 1969.

PLATT, ANTHONY M., ed., *The Politics of Riot Commissions: 1917–1970: A Collection of Official Reports and Critical Essays.* New York: The Macmillan Co., 1971.

PORAMBO, RON, *No Cause for Indictment: An Autopsy of Newark.* New York: Holt, Rinehart & Winston, 1971.

RAINWATER, LEE, *Behind Ghetto Walls: Black Families in a Federal Slum.* Chicago, Ill.: Aldine-Atherton, 1970.

RAINWATER, LEE, and WILLIAM L. YANCEY, *The Moynihan Report and the Politics of Controversy.* Cambridge, Mass.: The M.I.T. Press, 1967.

REIMERS, DAVID M., *White Protestantism and the Negro.* New York: Oxford University Press, 1965.

RITCHIE, BARBARA, *The Riot Report.* New York: The Viking Press, 1969.

ROCHE, JOHN P., *The Quest for the Dream.* New York: The Macmillan Co., 1963.

ROSE, ARNOLD M., *Race Prejudice and Discrimination.* New York: Alfred A. Knopf, 1951.

ROSSI, PETER H., ed., *Ghetto Revolts.* Chicago, Ill.: Aldine-Atherton, 1970.

SAUTER, VAN GORDON, and BURLEIGH HINES, *Nightmare in Detroit.* Chicago, Ill.: Henry Regnery Co., 1968.

SCHEER, ROBERT, ed., *Eldridge Cleaver: Post-Prison Writings and Speeches.* New York: Random House, 1969.

SCOTT, ANDREW M., et al., *Insurgency.* Chapel Hill, N.C.: University of North Carolina Press, 1970.

SEGAL, RONALD, *The Race War.* New York: The Viking Press, 1966.

SEIGENTHALER, JOHN, *Search for Justice.* Nashville, Tenn.: Aurora Publishers 1971.

SENATE SELECT COMMITTEE ON PENAL INSTITUTIONS, *Upgrading Correctional Manpower.* Sacramento, Calif.: California State Legislature, 1972.

SERVIN, MANUEL P., *The Mexican-Americans: An Awakening Minority.* Beverly Hills, Calif.: Glencoe Press, 1970.

SHARKANSKY, IRA, *Regionalism in American Politics.* Indianapolis, Ind.: The Bobbs-Merill Co., 1970.

STEADMAN, ROBERT F., ed., *The Police and the Community.* Baltimore, Md.: The Johns Hopkins Press, 1972.

STRAUS, FRANCES, *Where did Justice Go? The Story of the Giles-Johnson Case.* Boston, Mass.: Gambit, 1970.

SULLIVAN, DAVID S., and MARTIN J. SATTLER, *Revolutionary War: Western Response.* New York: Columbia University Press, 1971.

TASK FORCE ON ASSASSINATION AND POLITICAL VIOLENCE, *Assassination and Political Violence.* Washington, D.C.: U.S. Government Printing Office, 1969.

TUCKER, STERLING, *Beyond the Burning.* New York: Association Press, 1968.

TURNER, FREDERICK JACKSON, *The Significance of Sections in American History.* Reprint of 1932 ed. Gloucester, Mass.: Peter Smith, 1959.

WAGLER, CHARLES, and MARVIN HARRIS, *Minorities in the New World.* New York: Columbia University Press, 1958.

WASKOW, ARTHUR I., *From Race Riot to Sit-In: 1919 and the 1960's.* Garden City N.Y.: Doubleday & Co., 1966.

WHITEHEAD, DON, *Attack on Terror: F.B.I. Against the KKK in Mississippi.* New York: Funk & Wagnalls, 1970.

WIDICK, B. J., *Detroit: City of Race and Class Violence.* Chicago, Ill.: Quadrangle Books, 1972.

WILSON, JAMES Q., *Negro Politics: The Search for Leadership.* New York: The Macmillan Co., 1960.

———, *Varieties of Police Behavior: The Management of Law and Order in Eight Communities.* Cambridge, Mass.: Harvard University Press, 1968.

WOODWARD, VANN C., *The Strange Career of Jim Crow.* New York: Oxford University Press, 1966.

WRIGHT, NATHAN JR., *Ready to Riot.* New York: Holt, Rinehart & Winston, 1968.

WRIGHT, THEON, *Rape in Paradise.* New York: Hawthorn Books, 1966.

YOUNG, RICHARD P., *Roots of Rebellion.* New York: Harper & Row, Publishers, 1970.

Index of Cases *

*By common name

Index